Management Compensation in High Technology Companies

Management Compensation in High Technology Companies

Assuring Corporate Excellence

Jay Schuster

LexingtonBooks
D.C. Heath and Company
Lexington, Massachusetts
Toronto

Library of Congress Cataloging in Publication Data

Schuster, Jay.
  Management compensation in high technology companies.

  Bibliography: p.
  Includes index.
  1. Executives—Salaries, pensions, etc.—United States. 2. High technology
industries—United States. I. Title.
HD4965.5.U6S39   1984   621.381'7'0683   83–48703
ISBN 0–669–07395–4

Second printing, March 1984

Published simultaneously in Canada

Printed in the United States of America

International Standard Book Number: 0–669–07395–4

Library of Congress Catalog Card Number: 83–48703

For Judy

Contents

Preface

The idea for the investigation that resulted in this book occurred to me a number of years ago, when some associates and I were discussing company performance and how to measure and improve it. The subject was not new to us; we had discussed it many times before. Although we believed one important factor played a crucial role in the successful operating of a company—and its absence might account for a company's failing—we had no concrete substantiation of the soundness of our theory. I decided to do something about that.

Why are some companies profitable and innovative while others struggle to manage the resources they have, often with less than satisfactory results? Why are some companies' employees proud of their organizations and happy in their jobs, while other companies' employees are dissatisfied with and unsure of their roles? Although the poorer performers may be able to trace their financial problems to changes in the market demand for their products or services, instead of to any specific management action they may have taken, their employees may report a lack of internal communications, continuous internal strife, and excessive conflict within their work units or within their company as a whole. Surely these companies' internal problems cannot be separated fully from their problems in the market place. How could their corporate performance be improved? What is the secret of success?

My associates and I believed that companies that perform well have some common features. The most successful and profitable organizations have key leaders (or top executives) who are in touch with what is going on in their companies and in the business world. These executives are active in their businesses' operations, and they have a strong commitment to a series of essential, and fairly specific, management performance principles. The principles—or strong performance values (SPVs)—are applied continually in day-to-day management and decision making. The SPVs are so well communicated (and understood) that they have become a part of these companies' cultures, creating within each firm a strong performance value culture (SPVC).

The SPVs emphasize such essential business elements as profit and technical performance. More important than general slogans or broad statements of business strategy and mission, the SPVs are adapted and kept current through continuing communications as business circumstances change so that their cultural emphasis on long-range financial performance is never lessened. The SPVs are kept flexible and are designed to anticipate what will happen next.

The successful companies develop and reinforce management behavior that is consistent with their SPVCs through the sound design of administrative systems. One important administrative system is the management reward program, which defines and calls attention to good performance by communicating both intrinsic strokes and by granting financial rewards. Such a reward program helps all participants to feel good about being members of the company; it inspires a team effort approach among employees. In this way, the reward program contributes to the attainment and maintenance of the SPVC.

In our discussions about company performance, my associates and I stressed the importance of a company culture that is managed by SPVs. The investigation that served as the foundation of this book (see the appendix) was designed to evaluate whether our beliefs had any merit. We had talked about the importance of a strong performance-driven culture for so long that I thought it was time to find out whether culture really does have an impact on how companies perform. This book, then, is about the study of company culture and its implications for key leaders who want their companies to perform better financially.

The target of the book is the key leader—the person who runs a company, who sets management policy, determines company culture, and inspires organizational performance. To improve company performance, a key leader must initiate the changes that are necessary. Unless he or she not only is supportive but also is actively in pursuit of such change, little improvement will be achieved.

Because information on the design of compensation plans is included, this book also may be useful to individuals who recommend management compensation programs to key leaders. Today, many key leaders view management compensation as a fairly dismal art form. Only a few of the most successful companies attempt to match their financial reward programs to their own specific corporate cultures. Most firms copy what others do in the area of management compensation. This copy-cat practice helps to sustain the lead that very successful companies have in this area.

A lot of people helped to formulate the ideas that led first to the investigation and then to this book. Most important are the many managers and executives in the high technology companies who talked to me and other investigators for hours. These leaders spoke to us about their organizations' performance, entrepreneurship, values, cultures, and reward systems. They were frank and patient, and they made the entire research effort enjoyable. Many of these men and women will see their ideas in this book. A great many will not know how much they helped us to stay on the right track.

The work team that helped to develop the concepts and gather the information included Mary Brown and Tom Banks, who stayed with the study from the start until the finish, and Betty Freeman and Bill Gould, who joined us when we were in need of help and who gave us new and valuable insights. These four people kept me on my toes during the investigation.

Over the years, a number of people contributed to the development of the ideas presented here. Nate Winstanley, my original mentor, has always provided excellent perspectives concerning reward systems. More recently, David Cichelli contributed many good ideas during the numerous sessions held to "noodle through" the concepts of culture, values, and rewards. My wife, Judy, helped make me think about the ideas in as clear a fashion as I am capable. She has always made my culture worthwhile, and this book is for her, most of all.

1 Introduction

High technology companies are involved in the financial exploitation of scientific research in the areas of chemistry, physics, mechanics, electronics, medicine, biology, genetics, and learning. They are involved in the development of new materials, processes, devices, and systems for use in previously established or new practical applications, including those in electronic technology, the control of industrial processes, radar, computer technology, the production of artificial alloys and plastics, the manufacturing of food products, and agriculture. In short, high technology companies are in the business of taking advantage of rapid scientific progress.

High technology products and services are used throughout the world. The computer, for example, has enabled many industries to operate more efficiently and effectively by streamlining formerly cumbersome business processes. The United States and other developed countries have become heavily dependent on creative technology for innovation and productivity.

Background of the Industry

High technology industry has grown rapidly since the 1970s. As one of the new basic industries in the United States, it provides many jobs, as well as exciting ideas. In the 1980s, the economic strength of the country will rely more and more on high technology. The technology business has become essential to the economic leadership and strength of the United States.

In the past few years, other countries have advanced technologically, narrowing the U.S. lead to a point where the United States faces a possibly dangerous situation. Many people make a lot of money out of high technology, including the venture capitalists who back the companies, the stockholders who invest in the compnaies, and the executives, managers, scientists, and other employees who derive their livelihood from the companies. The success of the United State's competition for business in the world economy will depend, in large measure, on the products and services of its high technology companies.

The people in high technology are the true innovators. At this very moment, groups of high technology managers and scientists are starting

1

their own companies. Having learned their trade from previous employers, they are ready to capitalize on their experience. These entrepreneurs operate in a dynamic business environment, where a competitive advantage can depend on something as vulnerable and fragile as an idea, and they are changing the source of strength in the United States's economy. Their propensity toward innovation, coupled with their economic importance to the country, make these high technology people and their companies worthwhile objects of study in the areas of culture, organizational effectiveness, and management performance.

The key leaders in high technology must be able to respond to the demands of a rapidly changing business environment. The advantages one company has over another can be eliminated very quickly; competition among companies is keen. The key leaders are finding that the old concepts of management do not work for them, given their industry's increased dependence on innovation. The best of the key leaders are applying what they can from classical and contemporary management theories and designing new management practices to ensure that employees are highly motivated and satisfied—the best way to ensure, in turn, that their companies are successful.

These new management practices affect not only the industry's well-being but also the welfare of communities. Many communities across the United States have become financially healthy as a result of the success of a nearby high technology company or a business center that attracts such companies. The Silicon Valley in the West and Route 128 in the East provide examples of the impact these organizations have on communities. A loss of high technology leadership will cost the United States dearly. Although now an exporter of technology and its products and services, unless this leadership is maintained, the United States may become an exporter of food products and little else. Other countries are catching up rapidly to the United States's lead in technology. Improved productivity and financial performance in U.S. high technology companies is imperative if the country is to retain its competitive advantage.

Performance Improvement Is Important

The financial performance of all types of organizations can be improved significantly by their adoption of the management principles presented here. The high technology companies have grown rapidly and are at a critical point in their development. It is no longer possible for these organizations to do well in spite of ineffective management. Management performance makes a significant and measurable difference in the success of a company.

To show how the application of appropriate management principles is important to the performance of an organization, it is necessary to investigate both organizations that are performing very well and those that are not. Unless this is done, the relevant relationship between management principles and financial performance cannot be demonstrated. Thus, the study that served as the basis for this book investigated not only successful companies but also companies that are not performing as well.

The contention here is that strong performance values (SPVs) are essential to the financial success of a company. This contention is supported by the study's finding that SPVs are present only in the most profitable high technology companies. SPVs were not found in the organizations that do less well financially. As a result, the existence of SPVs can be identified as a significant determinant of the healthy financial performance of a company.

In addition, to reach a conclusion about the importance of strong performance values, as many other organizational variables as possible must be held constant. The most profitable and the least profitable high technology companies have much in common. They are members of a homogeneous industry that emphasizes the entrepreneur, and both companies that perform very well and those that perform less than well can be readily identified as demonstrating entrepreneurship. Both the most and least profitable companies also tend to have streamlined decision-making processes. Committees are not used extensively in management decision making, and the process of evaluating alternatives and reaching a decision (whether correct or incorrect) is speedy. Thus, neither entrepreneurship nor rapid decision making necessarily contribute to the success of a company.

Because the high technology industry depends on people for its success, all the companies value and nurture their employees' contributions and participation. The difference between good and poor performance lies in the quality of the employees' contributions. No matter how involved employees are in the generation of ideas, if the ideas generated do not lead to increased profits, extensive employee participation cannot be cited as a contributor to substantial organizational success. It is the quality of the participation, not the participation itself, that can be cited as a contributing factor—and as a variable that must be studied.

Both the most successful and the least successful companies have streamlined organizational structures. A few key people run the entire organization, and reporting relationships are clear. The size of the organizations probably has an impact on the extent to which control is exercised by the key leader. In the larger companies, the top executives reserve a few important decision areas for themselves, while the many other important business decisions are made at lower organizational levels. As is true with employee participation, with decision making, quality is the important variable. In the less successful companies, the quality of the decisions, and not where they are made, is the problem. One reason the most profitable companies are financially successful is because the decisons made by these companies' managers are sound, based on an understanding of the high technology industry. Although other companies may know their industry well, too, their managers are unable to apply this knowledge to the decisions they make.

In the final analysis, although all high technology companies share certain variables, such as entrepreneurship, employee participation, and streamlined decision-making processes and organizational structures, only the best of the corporate performers share strong performance values. The key to success, then, is the application of strong performance values in management practices. Companies with SPVs also seem to have employees that make sound decisions and generate profitable ideas—and perhaps that is not a coincidence.

Communicating Strong Performance Values

The most profitable high technology companies effectively communicate SPVs throughout their organizations. Successful communication of SPVs results in the creation of a strong performance value culture (SPVC). By encouraging people in their organizations to talk about the strong performance values and make them a part of their daily business lives, such companies spawn an atmosphere or culture where those characteristics that foster good performance predominate.

A company's administrative system communicates that company's values and priorities. Good administrative systems communicate SPVs by supporting face-to-face communications throughout the organization. Those systems or programs that communicate procedural priorities in ways that hinder rather than aid internal communications do not contribute to (and may discourage) employees' striving to improve performance.

Many profitable companies use financial rewards as a means of communicating the importance of SPVs. The best corporate performers associate their management compensation programs with the SPVs. In each of these companies, the management compensation plans (base salary and incentives) can be traced to the strong performance values of the firm's key leader. The best key leaders use the management compensation program as a tool of communication to show people how to perform better, not as a punitive system that distributes financial rewards on the basis of criteria over which the employees have little or no influence. Management compensation plans that communicate SPVs, then, can be said to contribute to good corporate financial performance in a significant way.

Although all management compensation programs tend to relate, in some measure, financial rewards to employee performance, the programs in the most profitable high technology companies are designed to reward performance that results in both qualitative and quantitative success. The primary aim of all organizations—profit—may not be the immediate outcome of current employee performance. For example, those technical and scientific contributions that cannot be measured quantitatively now but that may substantially boost profits in the future should be rewarded now. Compensation programs must reward current performance by identifying (with the help of the company's long- and short-term goals) employees' technological and business innovations, even those innovations that do not result in immediate financial gains.

The less profitable companies' management compensation programs tend to emphasize only end results rather than the attainment of interim goals along the way to success. They do not consistently communicate the importance of the SPVs in achieving a satisfactory bottom line in both the long and short term. What less profitable organizations do not seem to recognize is what good performance in the high technology industry means: although innovations result in profits, they result from people working together cooperatively and creatively. Because a project may take years to complete, those employees who contribute to the completion of each step or part of the project should be rewarded for that achievement.

The companies with long-standing management compensation plans are among the group that generates the least satisfactory financial results over the long and short term. The high technology industry is dynamic; no administrative system can stay fully responsive for long in such an environment. Therefore, management reward systems must be adjusted to meet the changing needs of their organizations. Not only must companies start with good compensation plan designs, but they also must adapt the designs to their specific business needs. As their needs change, so should their compensation programs.

Thus, the most successful companies change their management compensation programs when the programs no longer measure success accurately. In this industry, longevity is not an indication that a program is working. Programs should be evaluated on how well they communicate SPVs; if a management compensation program is not communicating the company's values and priorities, it should be changed.

High Technology and U.S. Economic Strength

During the current worldwide technological revolution, it is essential that the United States sustain its leadership in the development and sale of technological products and services. As the experiences in the auto and steel industry have shown, once a leadership position is lost, it is very difficult to regain. The United States is counting on its high technology industry to salvage its position of business leadership, or at least competitiveness. If other U.S. industries come to depend on high technology that is totally imported, the United States will be vulnerable to the vagaries of international politics and trade policies.

The performance stakes are high, then, in both absolute and relative terms. In absolute terms, the United States is concerned with staying on the leading edge of technological innovation. Retaining leadership in this area is important to the nation as a whole. In relative terms, each company within the industry wants to compete effectively.

High technology companies, like companies in other industries, vary in profit performance. Management practice is an important variable in the profit performance equation. How well the key leader communicates SPVs and rewards performance that is consistent with those values determines whether his or her company has a strong performance culture, which determines, in turn, how well the company does financially.

2 Performance Values and Company Culture

A company's culture determines how it, as an organization, relates to internal and external variables. The most successful high technology companies have cultures that are based on specific strong performance values. The performance values are established by the company's top executive, continuously communicated throughout the company by all managers, and reinforced by the effective design of administrative systems, such as management-compensation programs.

All organizations have cultures. People within a culture share the same outlooks, behavior norms, attitudes, and values. They have characteristic responses to situations. These shared basic values, norms, and responses form the foundation of the culture. Within an organization, some of these values define the characteristics of successful performance, the criteria that will be used to measure how well the company is doing, and the goals that should be sought by members of the organization.

Employees must behave in accordance with the cultural norms of their organization. In order to make any effective contribution to the organization, they must thoroughly understand the company's strong performance values. To ensure that their performance values are well communicated, the most successful companies reinforce behavior that is consistent with performance values through their reward systems. Among the most potent forms of reward a company can grant are those of a financial nature. Because of this, designing an effective compensation program is an essential step toward achieving successful performance, both of employees and of the organization as a whole. Well-designed financial rewards that communicate SPVs make a critical contribution to the future performance of the company.

Weak Performance Values

Just as a strong performance value culture contributes to the success of one company, weak performance values (WPVs) and a weak performance value culture (WPVC) contribute to the poor performance or failure of another company. Many of the less-than-successful companies have slogans about

7

organizational performance and objectives rather than performance values. These slogans do little to help the companies' leaders get the financial results they want; they do not make the same contribution that performance values do to shaping the companies' cultures and, hence, overall performance.

Characteristics and Results

Companies with weak performance value cultures (WPVCs) have no consistent performance values that are reinforced and communicated throughout their organizations. If people in these organizations are asked what their company is about, their answers will not reflect homogeneous strong performance values. In these companies, it is not possible to identify clearly what the organizations' leaders view as important to success because there are no consistent values that state such criteria.

In some instances, the top executive may have very good performance values but does not manage the company in a way that effectively and consistently emphasizes those performance values. Organizations with WPVCs tend to place much emphasis on individual employee performance, usually because the key leaders believe that high technology organizations are built on individual contributions. Often, these leaders have made significant individual contributions to the success of their companies and this remains their criterion for evaluation. The rewards in these organizations are given mostly on the basis of end results. Individual managers are evaluated according to how much impact he or she had on some profit-making project. The final measure of performance, then, is financial.

In a high technology environment, however, it is very difficult to single out individual contributions. Thus, in the organizations where managers are told to reward individual performance, they are not able to measure it effectively. Trying to attribute a measurable contribution to a specific individual generates strife and often results in employees' being hesitant to work as members of a team and to share the fruits of their efforts with others. In organizations that emphasize only individual performance, there is no teamwork. If one person has the solution to another person's problem, the person with the solution is not encouraged to share it because the company's culture stresses individual contributions, not cooperation. Consequently, good ideas are not shared, and internal competition for strokes and financial rewards adds to the strife.

When not based only on the evaluation of individual contributions, poor corporate performers' management compensation plans may be adaptations of plans used by high-visibility companies. The Xerox plan, the Hewlett-Packard plan, and the Control Data plan have been copied by many other organizations. In most instances, the copies have been poor translations of the originals, but the copying companies often feel their plans are good because they are based on a plan used by a well-known firm. This copy-cat behavior occurs because of the proliferation of compensation surveys in the high technology industry. In companies with WPVCs, compensation survey information is used not as a starting point for the design of a compensation plan that reflects the specific needs but as a testimonial for whatever compensation programs the companies are trying to adopt. What industry leaders do is a powerful predictor of what poor performers will do.

The Communications Factor

In organizations with WPVCs, the informal and formal communications channels often are clogged with information that is directed toward finding out what the organization is trying to accomplish. Communications channels are full of questions, but they offer few helpful answers. As a result, managers spend much of their time trying to determine what manner of performance would be consistent with the values of the key leader. The key leader, on the other hand, is trying to figure out why the employees are not doing what he or she would like them to do.

In companies with SPVCs, the key leaders use the strong performance values to communicate with their employees. They employ administrative systems to disseminate those values. Companies with WPVCs either do not communicate values through their administrative systems or they do so poorly. Their management compensation programs, for example, may be failing to effectively communicate the organizations' priorities.

Although many of the WPV companies encourage the documentation of communications in writing—and executives and managers in such companies tend to write a great many memos—much of the documentation either serves only to protect the writer from being assigned responsibility for something or is ambiguous in content. People do not talk to each other very much. The key leaders in a number of the companies that are performing less than satisfactorily communicate with their managers only through memos. Oral communications are limited to social subjects, while the exchange of business information and ideas is limited to written communications. When managers and top executives do meet, it usually is for the presentation of formal reports of business, technical, or financial progress, not for the exchange of ideas.

Once again, what is missing is management teamwork. WPVCs do not encourage employees to explore ideas or solve problems as a team. These managers identify themselves more closely with their professions than with their companies. In the high technology industry, employees' identification with their companies is all important. When teamwork is not emphasized effectively and managers and employees do not willingly exchange information concerning mutual problems or programs, overall company performance is bound to be poor.

Administrative Procedures

The companies that are performing less than satisfactorily use their administrative systems (policies and procedures) to manage the company rather than as supportive communications tools. The administrative procedures often replace face-to-face contact between executives and managers and, subsequently, between managers and the employees.

As are compensation programs, many administrative systems are adapted from systems originally created by a company that is viewed as a leader in the field. Companies that adopt systems often do not consider whether the systems are appropriate for their organizations. This is "me too" management, and its principle seems to be that, if a program is good enough for a company that is doing well, it must be good for other organizations, too. In many cases, one company's administrative programs in marketing, planning, training, and compensation are copies of another highly visible company's programs. However, copying companies should realize that dressing up to look like someone famous does not make you famous.

Unlike their programs, the SPVs of the successful companies are not being copied or transplanted. Policies and procedures are designed to correspond with the features of a company's culture; transplanting the policies and procedures to another company will not result in the culture's being transplanted as well. It is the SPVC of a successful company that other firms should be copying, not its procedures.

Management Succession

To sustain their good performance, successful companies must have new key leaders who are committed to continuous management by performance values prepared to take over from current leaders when necessary. In companies with weak performance values, little or no attempt is made to prepare members of the current management team to assume the key leader position. Because of this, these companies' cultures may change substantially each time a new leader assumes control. This change can benefit company performance only in the instance where the old culture supported poor profit performance.

Mixed Performance Values

Most companies have mixed performance value cultures (MPVCs) with mixed performance values (MPVs). There are many more companies in this category than there are the previous categories, and the managers and employees in these companies often experience the most difficulty in identifying their organizations' priorities.

Characteristics and Results

It is fairly easy to determine whether an organization has a weak or a strong performance value culture. In the case of an organization with a mixed performance value culture, however, the signals its leaders give can indicate a strong performance value culture at one time and a weak performance value culture at another.

In the absence of strong leadership, managers may lead a company in a variety of diverse directions. If a company does not promote strong performance values, there will be a gap in the organization. In a company with a weak performance value culture, that gap is filled with confusion. In a company with a mixed performance value culture, the gap is filled, not by the key leader's strong performance values, but by the performance values of other powerful individuals in the company. The problem with this is that these performance values will not be uniform and integrated, and so they may not be clear to the employees.

The Communications Factor

In a company with an MPVC, the key leader's performance values do not permeate the organization. The effects of this situation are similar to the effects of a WPVC, where the leader's strong performance values are not communicated throughout the organization. In the company with MPVs, the cadre of executives near the key executive are not communicating the key leader's performance values, but some may be communicating their own performance values and others may be communicating a complete lack of performance values. Because these performance values may differ from executive to executive, they usually lack the integration that the key leader in an SPVC gives them.

A good example is a high technology company in the Midwest, where the key leader does not communicate his performance values. However, the organization's marketing executive communicates his strong performance values, which emphasize market penetration and increased sales performance quite well. The chief technical executive also communicates strong performance values, which indicate that technical quality is all important, and, in manufacturing, the top executive emphasizes cost control. None of the executives' strong performance values are integrated or coordinated, and because such values may contradict each other in some situations, they can only confuse employees.

The top executive in a company with an MPVC has, intentionally or unintentionally, delegated the responsibility for management to the other executives. Their performance values, or lack of performance values, dominate and confuse the managers in the company. The only good thing about this type of culture is that some strong performance values may exist, even though they are not well integrated. If an executive who can communicate his or her strong performance values throughout the company should succeed the present key leader, the company's culture would become an SPVC and company performance would be strengthened.

Executives and managers in high technology companies that are performing well direct most of their energy toward issues that are relevant to technology and the business and not toward inspiring internal competition for rewards and attention. The political strife and internal conflict that exist in a company with a WPVC also exist in a company with an MPVC. Because some units within a company with a MPVC have performance values that are not coordinated with those of other units in the company, and because some units have no communicated performance values, factions exist, and these factions pull and tug for power and influence. In such companies, employees expend more energy on fighting internal power struggles than on conducting the business of the company. Where good communications channels do exist, they are used to direct influence within the company rather than to expand company sales or develop a new product or service. People do not work well across organizational boundaries, and individuals, groups, and entire departments become compartmentalized. This is not an environment where ideas are exchanged. Employees learn little, and teamwork is spotty at best. The company with an MPVC can become immobilized as a result of the lack of clearly communicated and reinforced strong performance values to which all executives subscribe.

Administrative Procedures

The companies with MPVCs tend to follow the latest management development or performance improvement fad. They go from sensitivity training to management by objectives and back again, seldom committing the organization to a single management technique long enough to give that technique a fair test. They follow the latest leader and copy what other companies are doing. Because their executives' values may vary, such companies may be applying several different procedures simultaneously, each in a different work unit. One major executive may be attempting to get his or her department into strategic planning while another may be saying that this approach is of no use to the organization. As a result, no procedures get a fair trial, much time and money is wasted, and the organization has no clearly identified administrative procedures.

For example, consider how different companies evaluate management performance. Good corporate performers use group performance criteria, while companies with weak performance values use programs that attempt to measure only individual performance. In a company with an MPVC, a great many approaches to performance evaluation can be found throughout the company. Such variety may have some benefits if each organizational unit has different problems and, in one unit, group performance standards are more accurate measures of performance while, in another unit, individual performance standards are more accurate measures. If this is the case, the variations in appraisal methods reflect the differences in the organization's needs and their application makes good sense.

However, when the units are in competiton with each other, their use of different performance evaluation methods can contribute to the internal strife. One executive may say that the performance review system another unit uses is inconsistent with what the company is all about, and the executive in charge of the other unit may claim the same thing is true of the system used by the unit supervised by the first executive. Caught in the middle is the manager who does not know what to do; the credibility of both executives, as well as of the management processes, is in jeopardy as a result of the conflict.

Management Succession

Usually the key leader position is the objective of the combatants in organizations with MPVs. Because the key leader often has not communicated the rules of the corporate promotion game, executives spend an excessive amount of time trying out behaviors they hope will position them in the succession stream. While the executives are experimenting with behaviors, there is much confusion in the rest of the organization. If a company does not have a succession plan that reflects the performance values of the organization, the continuity that management succession should provide is lost and the company is much less productive than it would be if promotional routes were clear.

In many cases, the key executive in a company with MPVs was, if not the founder, at least part of the organization when it was founded. However, unlike key leaders in companies with strong performance value cultures, the leader of a company with an MPVC does not recognize the importance of clearly communicated and reinforced performance values. Because of this, his or her organization will be in a potentially explosive situation if it should face business or technological adversity. Conflicting values and the lack of management teamwork fail to place the organization in a position where it can handle problems that threaten the overall performance of the company. The roots of the culture are volatile; when things are bad, people within the company expend energy trying to find out who is to blame rather than on solving the problems at hand.

The executives in a company with an SPVC are experienced in working as a management team. When external problems arise for their company, these leaders will use their habitual method to address the problems in a synergistic and coordinated manner. In a company with an MPVC, the executives spend a great deal of their time trying to figure out how to position themselves internally. When external problems arise, the executives also follow their habitual path: they look for people within the company to blame rather than for the solutions to real business and technical problems.

Strong Performance Values

A company must have strong performance values if it is going to sustain a high level of profitable performance. All cultures have either implicit or explicit values of one sort or another. In some companies, these values are as general as honesty and fair play. Other companies have values that are equally sloganlike; a general statement such as General Electric's "progress is our most important product" would be considered a value statement. The unwritten values of good business ethics, product quality, good employee relations, and the like are important contributors to an organization's culture; however, they are not strong performance values. Many organizations have these values and yet do not perform well. The profit performance of an organization is not directly related to the presence of these values. In many instances, companies that are performing quite poorly have very high-sounding, sloganlike values that state the organizations' dedication to corporate goals of great merit.

Strong performance values make specific contributions to the actual operation of the company. They need not be posted in the lobby to be an effective management tool. One company visited during the research phase of this book had some elaborate statements posted in the reception area. The statements would lead one to believe that this was a strong performance value driven organization; however, the statements were, in fact, a product of an interior decorator, and the chief executive had never paid any attention to them except as a decoration.

The most powerful strong performance values in high technology companies may not be posted anywhere. However, they permeate communications throughout the organization. Nearly everybody in a company with an SPVC can be questioned about the strong performance values of the company and will know what they are. More important, their descriptions will not come off as religious dogma. Rather, the employees will describe the SPVs in their own words, which indicates that they have internalized, rather than memorized, the strong performance values.

Characteristics and Results

The term *strong* is used to indicate that the values permeate the organization. They represent crucial priorities and have become a part of the financially successful organization's culture. Just having the performance values is not enough; they must be strong performance values, which can be traced throughout the organization and which are part of daily conversations and written documents.

The SPVs must consistently be part of a company's culture. In the most profitable companies, the SPVs have been in place for at least two years. All important management activities in these organizations are based on these strong performance values. SPVs are a part of the business planning process and the development of any statements of mission. They are considered when administrative systems are established, and they are reflected in the design of both financial and nonfinancial reward systems.

The strong performance values in the most profitable high technology companies are used by the key leaders to develop effective principal company goals, business strategies, objectives, and missions to help the companies attain their financial objectives. The strong performance values of those high technology companies that perform most successfully can be classified in six areas: (1) profit performance; (2) technical excellence; (3) competitive advantage; (4) responsiveness to customers and environment; (5) employee contributions; and (6) community responsibilities.

These are the six strong performance values that characterize a strong performance value culture. The first one, profit performance, generally is identified as an end result of success in the other strong performance value areas. The organizations that perform well recognize that doing well in other performance value areas will result in profit. Hence, profit performance is an incentive to achieve the other values.

Number One—Profit Performance. The profit performance value is defined in terms of both the long- and the short-term financial objectives of the company. Profit performance is a reflection of, for example, concrete improvement in net profits, increased or sustained return on assets, better cash flow, improvement in the financial worth of the company to its shareholders, an increased market share, or increased sales. Whatever measures or indicators a company uses to identify its financial success are the measures that indicate profit performance. Such measures often begin as financial objectives.

The most profitable companies recognize that setting financial objectives that suggest the companies want to achieve a high and sustained level of growth at any cost is folly. The key leaders of these companies assign modifiers to their financial performance values. They attach, for example, the concept of a quality product or service to the customer to the aim of profit growth. In this way, the key leaders are answering the question, growth at what cost, in terms their employees can understand. They are not communicating to their people that all they want is to succeed financially; instead, they are making it clear to everyone that, with profit, another value is to be achieved.

This emphasis on quality is of critical importance. The profit SPV is the bottom line of the total management effort. It communicates to the people in the company that the organization is in business to make a profit. However, because financial success should never be communicated as an all-important value, and because no business will last long if it does not offer a usable and dependable product or service, quality or a similar value is attached to the profit SPV. The leaders communicate, then, that profit is to be made, but not at the expense of quality.

Number Two—Technical Excellence. All of the best corporate performers in the high technology industry indicate that technical excellence is a performance value they will not sacrifice for profit. Technical excellence is a modifier and condition of sustained financial growth. The companies' key leaders correlate this value with continued progress and believe, rightfully so, that the development of useful and marketable technology is the source of any long-term financial success their companies may have. These leaders will not sacrifice the ideas and innovations that lead to technical excellence in order to achieve a good short-range financial posture.

This strong performance value area describes what the organization will do to stay on the leading edge of its chosen technical field(s) or identifies what it will do to catch up with the leader. When communicated to employees, this SPV should provide detailed guidance concerning what steps are necessary to enter a specific field or to develop a new or modified product or service.

Technical excellence is, essentially, the SPV for product development. It indicates where a company wants to be (competitively) in a technical area, although it does not state any confidential information that could be of use to other firms in the field that are interested in knowing what that company is planning to do. Thus, although this SPV has to be detailed enough to get its message across to employees, it cannot be so detailed that it tips the company's hand to competitors. Simply saying, "we will be excellent technically," is inadequate. That is a banal slogan, which, unfortunately, may be the way companies that are not doing well in the high technology industry are stating their values.

Number Three—Competitive Advantage. Competitive advantage is the result of a combination of technical innovation and strong marketing. All key leaders are cognizant of their competitors. However, only executives in the companies that are performing poorly are overly worried about their competitors' progress. In a successful company, this SPV compares what the company is doing to what it believes competitors are doing and indicates how it is going to improve its position. In the very good corporate performers, the SPV is stated in an active rather than a defensive way. It states that key leaders are going to do something and that they have a plan that outlines how they will do it. In most cases, a business strategy or plan is integrated with this SPV.

The action the company is going to take is expressed in terms of attaining or maintaining a leadership position in a specific area of business through a combination of marketing strategy and technological innovation. The SPV indicates how a competitor's market will be penetrated or how an untapped market will be explored and exploited. The SPV outlines how business competitors will be approached (either by confrontation or avoidance methods). The competitive-advantage SPV should reflect a good understanding of the organization's strengths and weaknesses. It is not as detailed as a marketing projection or a sales plan. Instead, it deals generally with the known facts and the possible alternatives available to the organization.

Number Four—Response to Customers and Environment. The SPV that states the company's response to customers and environment is a definition of the market in which the company competes and the business and technological environments that this market is in. In most instances, this SPV includes information that projects how the market will change over the long and short terms, what the company will do to influence the market, and the role environmental variables will play in the company's ability to respond effectively to the realities of the market and its environments.

The response to customers and environment is the SPV that communicates to employees the importance of the customer and the necessity to remain ever alert to the rapidly changing business and technological environment. This SPV suggests the appropriate way to learn about a customer's problems or plans and how to integrate this information in the company's decision-making processes. It represents, so to speak, the intelligence section of the organization. In short, this SPV states how the company diagnoses customer needs and the business environment so that the key leaders and executives do not lose touch with what is going on in the markets in which the company sells its products or services.

For this SPV to be achieved, the company's key leader and executives must be in a position to predict and respond to changes that impact the company's business. It requires their keeping in touch with sociological and psychological changes in all the markets the company serves as well as with the activities of competitors.

Number Five—Employee Contribution. Employee contribution recognizes the important roles managers and employees play in the attainment of other strong performance values. Often, this SPV acknowledges the contribution of both groups and individuals to the company. In the most successful companies, this SPV suggests how good contributors may increase their own financial worth as the company performs better, both technologically and financially.

Employee contribution is defined differently from company to company. In some companies, extensive employee participation is emphasized while, in others, a very streamlined decision-making process (so that the organization can respond quickly to a business opportunity or problem) is stressed. However the role of the employee is defined, a number of performance dimensions should be emphasized. The message the employee contribution SPV should communicate is that employees are what makes a company successful and they will share in the good things that happen to the company.

Number Six—Community Responsibilities. Key leaders of the companies with SPVCs believe that ethical business behavior is an important ingredient for success. These key leaders are concerned about how they are viewed as corporate citizens. All express a concern about how their companies are viewed by local, national, and, in some cases, international communities. The SPV of community responsibilities emphasizes both social and community responsibilities. Although some of the motives for achieving this SPV may be independent of the company's concerns about its profit performance, most of the motivation comes from the belief that a good organizational image is important to financial and technological success.

The root of the community responsibilities SPV, then, is the idea that being viewed as a good citizen (a good company to have in the community) will influence the customer's perception of that company. All other things being equal, the organization with the best reputation in the community is thought to have a business advantage. In turn, the companies that perform the best are the ones most often identified by their competitors as effective corporate citizens. This SPV defines the company's role as a member of the community in broad terms.

The Relationship between Strong Performance Values. All of the organizations with strong performance value cultures demonstrate that they are interested in performance that is consistent with all of the six SPVs. However, the organizations stress only two or three of the SPVs in their communications and mention the other strong performance values in terms of how they can be used to help attain the principal two or three performance values.

For example, when profit performance, competitive advantage, and technical excellence are the SPVs emphasized most in a high technology organization, a supportive relationship between these strong performance values and the other three SPVs is communicated to employees. Achieving the other three SPVs will help to achieve profit performance, technical excellence, and competitive advantage. This suggests that, in many companies with strong performance values, there are primary SPVs and secondary (or supportive) SPVs. Evidence shows that, when this relationship between values exists in a company, the company is likely to be successful.

The Communications Factor

Key leaders use the SPVs to communicate with the employees in their companies. This is the SPVs' principal purpose as a management tool. Although they may be used in the company's planning process and for other management functions, the main reason for their existence is to communicate what the company is trying to do. SPVs show employees how they fit in the broad corporate picture. They provide managers with evaluative criteria for judging possible solutions to business problems that are affecting group and individual behavior.

It is important to differentiate strong performance values from other customs that may be essential parts of a company's culture. Some organizations are participative in nature and encourage their employees to provide input to the management decision-making process; other organizations are hierarchical in nature and only permit executives to participate in the decision-making process. Both of these types of organizations will communicate their styles and perhaps other mores to their employees. In addition, both types may have strong performance values. The organizations' communications to employees should not confuse the SPVs with management styles or mores. Although the styles may utilize the SPVs and, in turn, the communication of the SPVs may strengthen or sustain the styles and other mores, the SPVs are not the same as management style and should not be presented as such to employees.

Administrative Procedures

The companies that are managed in the best way tinker with all types of administrative systems. As the discussion about compensation programs for managers will indicate later in this book, key leaders modify their organizations' reward systems to reflect the characteristics of their cultures. It is important to introduce this point here because it demonstrates, again, that the good corporate performers view an administrative system as a means to an end rather than as an end in and of itself. Good leaders use their compensation programs to communicate their companies' SPVs and to reinforce their SPVCs. These programs have no greater values than those.

Administrative systems should not interfere with the direct oral communications between managers, executives, and other employees. The compensation program, like other administrative systems, should not hinder the management of the company; it should be another management tool. Thus, compensation programs must be flexible so that they can be changed to meet varying management situations. If a compensation plan is not constantly evaluated on the basis of its ability to meet the needs of the company, and if it is not changed when it no longer meets those needs, it is not a useful tool for managers. The process of altering a compensation program—or tinkering with it—is a creative one and helps to keep top management in step with the needs of the organization.

Management Succession

The management succession plans of the organizations that perform best financially are very clear; only those executives who are instrumental in helping the key leader communicate and manage by means of the SPVs are in line for the key leader's job. Those executives and managers who behave in a manner that is inconsistent with the company's SPVs have little chance of job growth. More often than not, if such executives and managers hold positions that are essential to the communication of the SPVs throughout the organization (and most management positions are essential to this), they are removed from those positions.

The successful high technology companies use the SPVs to show executives and managers how to succeed in their companies. Very little destructive internal political activity is evident in such companies, and the resultant climates help the key leaders to direct the efforts of their management teams to those business and technical issues that are directly relevant to the success of their companies. Reporting relationships are clear, and the culture provides strong guidance concerning the route employees should follow for management and technical success.

In companies with SPVCs, key leaders have well-established plans of succession for the members of their organizations that are developed so that the leaders can be assured that the companies' SPVCs will be sustained after leaders leave. People who share the key leader's SPVs are in the direct line of management succession. Because the top management team's commitment to the SPVs is clear, the employees in these companies are less concerned about possible changes in management direction should their present key leaders leave.

Management succession should be planned so that the strong performance values and the culture that encompasses them on a continuing basis are both sustained. A management succession plan also indicates what manner of behavior will be reinforced and lead to promotions and other rewards. It presents a promotional picture and tells all employees what they must do to progress in the organization.

The Influence of Performance Values on Company Culture

Performance differs significantly from company to company and, in this fairly dynamic and homogeneous growing industry, the companies that manage through the use of strong performance values perform the best. No other organizational variable is a characteristic only of companies that succeed; other variables also may be features of the companies that perform poorly. The companies that do less well financially have either weak performance value cultures or mixed performance value cultures. This suggests that the strong performance values and the priorities they imply are important components of a company's financial performance.

Kinds of Company Culture

It is difficult to understand the character of an organization without knowing the logic applied in the selection of management compensation and other administrative programs. To gain this insight, the researchers who conducted the investigation that served as the basis for this book used a general system of cultural classification to see if any relationship existed between a company's culture, its values, and its approach to management compensation. Three classifications were used: strong performance value culture, weak performance value culture, and mixed performance value culture. One group of twenty-four organizations was identified as having strong performance value cultures. Researchers also identified a group of twelve companies as having weak performance value cultures and the remaining majority were classified as having mixed performance value cultures.

Among the companies investigated, the companies with strong performance value cultures experienced net profit performance over the last five years that far exceeded that of the other companies. Also, companies with SPVCs outperformed the other companies in terms of growth in earnings per share, cash flow, and nearly every other quantitative financial performance measure. Their better performance clearly was due to the key leaders' effective communication of the strong performance values. These companies' financial reward systems reinforced the strong performance values by communicating to managers and all other employees how they should perform to make the company do well. This was not the case in the other organizations.

In addition to conferences with key executives, the investigators talked to middle managers and professional staff. They also reviewed the available written information and administrative policies and procedures that discussed what the organizations were trying to accomplish. Such documents indicated the existence (or lack) of the thread running through the organizations that showed the degree of homogeneity of strong performance values, where the SPVs existed, and how they were being communicated.

Both formal communications channels and informal networks communicate information within an organization. By interviewing people at various levels within the company and studying formal documents, the investigators determined whether both communications systems were transmitting similar values. As the review of compensation practices will show, in companies with SPVCs, administrative systems and the informal and formal communications channels support homogeneous performance values.

Changing Company Culture to Accommodate Strong Performance Values

The key leaders of companies that perform the best financially use several management techniques to improve overall profit performance. These techniques include:

1. Establishing and reinforcing the strong performance values. Only the key leader, with the help of executives, can define or modify a company culture.
2. Establishing administrative systems, such as management compensation programs. Having established the SPVs, the key leader must communicate and reward performance that is consistent with them. Admin-

istrative systems are used to support the SPVC and communicate the SPVs throughout the company.

3. Building a cadre of supportive senior executives. These executives help the key leader to reinforce the SPVC by training other managerial personnel throughout the company to communicate the SPVs and behave in accordance with them. Executives who do not support the company's SPVC must be replaced.

4. Establishing a clear path to be followed for managerial success. Everyone must understand that maintaining the SPVs is a priority and the best way to get ahead in the company.

5. Remaining responsive to changes in the technological and business environments in which the company operates. The company's culture must be adapted as the company's needs change. This requires nurturing the SPVC on a continuing basis.

Effectively changing culture is not a simple task. It requires the presence of a key leader who is willing to follow the guidelines just listed. Establishing an SPVC, however, appears to be worth the problems in the case of high technology companies. The problems of cultural change will be referred to again from time to time in the book; the importance of cultural change cannot be overstressed.

Research results support the idea that performance values must be established initially at the top of the company. In addition, managers and employees must talk about the SPVs, and the values must be part of (reflected in) long-term goals, operational plans, and financial and nonfinancial reward systems. Because performance related values help to orient people within the organization's culture and tell them what is required of them, cultural clarity is important if the organization is to achieve good corporate performance.

New employees should be able to clearly identify the strong performance values of the company and the role individual workers play in attaining these values. By establishing specific administrative systems, executives will help the employees understand the company environment. By adapting such systems to changes in the business situation, they will keep the strong performance values up to date and enable members of the organization to choose the best strategy or tactic for any given situation.

The Role of Management

An effective top executive is essential to the success of a high technology company. The leaders' management styles may vary from one successful company to another, but all of the key leaders utilize strong performance values in their styles.

Although managers at all levels can help in the development of administrative systems to communicate SPVs, only the key leader can establish, and subsequently change, the SPVs because only he or she can determine which primary strong performance values will make the company successful.

In some cases, the key leader established the SPVs and the resulting strong performance value culture at the time he or she founded the company. In other cases, the key leader joined the organization later in its development, adapting the previous leader's SPVs, bringing SPVs from a prior place of employment, or developing the SPVs after assuming the key leader position.

In companies that have long performed successfully with the help of SPVs, the administrative systems are already in place and a new key leader may need only to adjust the systems to the new circumstances. When the new leader brings SPVs with him or her or develops them, he or she may need to substantially modify the existing administrative systems or create new ones that reflect the SPVC.

The key leader cannot manage by SPVs without assistance from all levels of management. Without supportive executives who assist in the management communications process, the key leader will have difficulty establishing the main channels that communicate SPVs and the central management elements that sustain the SPVC. Usually, the executive group consists of a technical executive, a financial executive, a marketing and sales executive, a manufacturing executive, and a human resources executive. These executives provide the key leader with information about their areas of management, and they are responsible for ensuring that their parts of the organization operate in accordance with the SPVC. The functional executives must cooperate with each other to ensure that the company is managed in a consistent way that reflects the performance values. The development of a good executive team is central to the profitable workings of a high technology company.

However, no leader can sit back and wait for his or her executives to report what is going on. The leader must "work the company" by being involved in what is going on in the organization and by keeping in touch with what and how the company is doing. The most successful leaders make the SPVs work from a hands-on perspective and do not rely solely on others for information. Although they must take counsel and delegate many decisions, they must know what decisions have been made and how they have effected the operations.

The Role of Administrative Systems

Administrative systems are those formal and informal methods managers use to get something done. They set policy and procedure for a wide range of activities, from the preparation of technical reports to the presentation of marketing information and strategy, from the development of business and financial plans to the formulation of compensation programs. Many companies formalize their administrative systems as they grow. However, all policies and procedures should be well documented so that employees know the rules.

The nature of the administrative systems is important to the SPVC. Administrative systems must be associated with the SPVs and, in turn, the SPVs should be traceable throughout the administrative systems. The strong performance values must be reflected in all written materials that are distributed throughout the company.

In investigators' discussions with business people and academics about the role SPVs play in the management of a company, one question always came up. That question, whether SPVs are like business plans, strategies, or some sort of supergoals, may have reflected a problem with semantics. If a problem in semantics exists, it is because some companies call a goal or strategy a strong performance value. However, these are not the same. A business strategy does not intrinsically increase sales. A strategy that is applied effectively within an SPV and that defines the role increased sales play in the overall profit performance of the company can increase sales. Thus, strategies depend on previously established SPVs for their success.

All companies have business goals, missions, plans, or strategies that are important to the companies' operations, but these are seldom discussed by employees below the executive level because they are not intrinsically important to the employees. Administrative tools such as strategies, plans, and missions are useful for limited periods but are not part of the operating philosophy of the company (although they must reflect that philosophy). Because of this, they should be viewed as aids in the communication of SPVs within an SPVC. They are also important in helping to determine whether the strong performance values are being interpreted appropriately by employees, especially when the strategies themselves are attempts to adapt the organization to changes in the high technology environment. Administrative systems, then, are means to an end and are expendable, while the SPVC is an end in and of itself and is not expendable.

One important administrative system is the management compensation program. The employee contributions SPV should communicate that effective group performance is central to the overall successful performance of the company. No high technology organization can rely on individuals, working alone, for success. This business is too complex and too dependent on the generation of ideas. Teamwork is the best route to organizational success, and all employees must be able to contribute as members of a team, sharing their ideas and helping each other in the process of innovation. Individual contributions are critical to the success of a work unit only if they are integrated within the unit. People who cannot function as a member of the team are of less importance to the company than are those who can work with others to solve problems. Because of this, management compensation programs and other reward systems should emphasize group performance whenever possible.

Gaining competitive business and technological advantages is an incremental process that takes time and coordinated effort. The strong financial performance values of the company can be attained if each step in the process is identified as important and its attainment is rewarded accordingly. Qualitative criteria, which are necessarily subjective in nature, should communicate the performance steps that must be taken to obtain the desired financial results. The use of qualitative performance objectives and criteria is not a scientific process. However, some performance cannot be measured by quantitative yardsticks and trying to measure it quantitatively may lead to inaccurate compensation judgments and behavior that is inconsistent with the long-term interests of the company. If quantitative criteria are communicated in the area of technological or engineering development, for instance, quality may be sacrificed so that employees can meet the numerical goal.

The qualitative evaluation of results may involve judging and rewarding performance retrospectively or on the basis of whether milestones, established to guide the efforts of a group in its search for the solution to a specific business or technological problem, have been attained. The use of milestones not only directs effort in a way that allows a considerable amount of leeway for the exploration of avenues that may appear more promising than the original route but also does not delay the awarding of appropriate compensation or other rewards to hard workers.

The Role of Communications Systems

Companies should have well-communicated statements of performance values. In organizations with weak performance value cultures, even if the chief executives have performance values essential to their firms' sustained performance, the values are not communicated, implicitly or explicitly, throughout the organization. In these cases, the chief executives may be the only ones who know the performance values. This lack of communication must change if these companies are to become more productive and profitable.

The difference between how unprofitable organizations are managed and how the more profitable companies are managed lies in their use of administrative systems and controls. In the profitable companies with SPVCs, administrative systems associate the methods to be used to get things done with the strong performance values. Corporate policies and procedures effectively communicate and expedite the attainment of the SPVs. For example, one effective policy states that a line manager should help interpret procedures for his or her specific work unit. In this way, the system is allowing for information gathering as well as setting a rule. It does not provide absolute answers, simply guidelines. All policies and procedures, whether general or specific, should be documented and periodically evaluated to make sure that the company is responding appropriately to current circumstances.

Administative systems must facilitate the communication and reinforcement of the strong performance values. Policies and procedures should not come between interactions of the key leader and the top executive group or the face-to-face dialogues between executives and managers and managers and subordinates. The systems also must not distort the SPVs. The accurate and effective transmission of SPVs helps the key leader run the company. Poorly designed administrative systems that inhibit the repetition of information that reinforces the high-performance culture or distorts the information contribute to reduced corporate performance.

In companies with WPVCs or MPVCs, the administrative systems often come between the key leaders and their subordinates because the procedures used provide little opportunity for face-to-face communications. In these companies, there is limited opportunity for information from the external world and information from lower levels within the companies to get through to the leaders. The people running the companies, therefore, are sheltered from occurrences within the organizations and those in the external environment. Without the help of administrative systems that channel information both upward and downward, companies cannot respond effectively to changes, whether external or internal. In a rapidly changing world, such poor response to business realities is bound to affect a company's credibility and, eventually, profitability.

Financial rewards that reinforce cooperation and teamwork communicate the desirability of such cooperation. Performance criteria, then, should include directions about how to work as a team member and should identify how individual contributions to the team effort will be measured and rewarded. In an industry where effective group performance is critical to success, measuring individual performance is a difficult proposition that can cause internal conflict and inequity. Most leaders in the high technology industry are more concerned with the performance of organizational units than they are with the performance of individuals. Thus, they should not be designing appraisal systems that measure the performance of employees as single contributors and that communicate the superiority of individual performance standards over group performance standards.

Although developing sustained teamwork is difficult, it is worth it to the bottom line. Getting people to work together well and to solve business and technical problems cooperatively depends on establishing performance values that stress the importance of communication. Group performance can be successful only if information is shared, between groups as well as within groups. Therefore, one measure of a team's effectiveness is the openness of its communications channels.

Having a written statement of organizational goals and objectives is an important part of a communications system. However, these goals should not be confused with strong performance values nor with cultural posturing. Such statements of values are ineffective if their stated objectives are not reflected in their companies' day-to-day operations. If these statements are simply copies of the objectives of other highly visible high technology organizations that do not apply to the copying firms' situations or if they are not communicated regularly throughout the sponsoring organizations, they are at best having no effect on employees' performance and at worst are confusing employees. Those values that are visible but not operational must be separated from those values that actually are used and communicated. Any written statement of goals must reflect the realistic and actual values of the company.

Summary

Organizations with the key leaders who communicate the strong performance values and establish strong performance value cultures tend to be among the most profitable companies. This suggests that companies that do not manage with SPVs will do less well financially. Research shows no other existing organizational or cultural variable that accounts for the difference in companies' financial performance. Because investigation indicates that company culture can be changed, this variable offers hope to the less successful organizations. Culture can be changed by the key leader's introduction of SPVs, and the managers' communication and reinforcement of them through the use of well-designed administrative systems. By making the strong performance values an integral part of the company culture, a key leader may improve profit performance in the long-term.

3 Management Compensation Today

Leaders of the top high technology companies believe that a management-compensation program should be designed to communicate and reward performance that is consistent with the strong performance values of the company. This means there is room for improvement in many companies' present management compensation programs, especially in the areas of short- and long-term incentives and job evaluation.

The thrust of this chapter, then, is the development and/or modification of management compensation plans that get the results the key leaders desire. When creating or modifying a compensation plan, it is important to determine the organization's needs, the logic behind the various available compensation programs, what areas within the company and what specific management responsibilities will be improved or hindered by which of the various compensation programs available, and how the chosen program can be related to the company's corporate culture. In particular, close attention should be paid to the methods used to determine management base salaries, short-term incentive plans, long-term incentive plans, perquisites, and special benefits.

Management's Present Concerns

All high technology companies have a management compensation program of some sort. The key leaders interviewed during the research period of this book all identified management compensation as an issue of importance to them. Nearly all of them felt that their current management compensation plans were not doing as complete a job as possible.

Those leaders who have established SPVCs in their organizations want management compensation plans that communicate and reinforce the SPVs much better than their current plans do. The key leaders of SPVC companies that perform well believe it is necessary to integrate the strong performance values of a company into its management compensation program. Some believe that their plans are doing this to a certain extent now, but tax and accounting regulations, which limit the creative alternatives available, hinder complete integration. Top executives in companies with WPVCs or

MPVCs are less sure of why they are uncomfortable with their compensation plans. Although these key leaders say they will make changes in their programs within the next year or so, most of them are unsure whether any type of program, especially an incentives-based one, can be designed to help them manage their companies better. Always willing to try new methods, all the executives nonetheless know that merely changing to a different plan will not be helpful unless the change is made in response to a recognized problem or need.

In high technology companies, the top business priority is responding quickly to the rapid growth in technology. An important part of this priority is keeping the existing technical staff up to date on current technology while bringing younger contributors into the company. Not only maintaining but also increasing the share of a growing market while staying profitable is, then, the critical business priority that management compensation programs must address. It is in this area that management compensation plans that reinforce SPVs can do the most good.

Management compensation plans must be designed to take the offensive in the high technology business. Many current programs merely help companies keep the market share they now have. As a result, key leaders, who are worried about keeping their firms and their employees up to date in a changing business and technical environment, are giving up on the idea that a management compensation program can make a contribution toward the achievement of their companies' top priority. Some executives are skeptical of the ability of management compensation plans to help them run their companies better, although they believe that such plans must be a part of the overall business plan and should do something more than just deal with tax and accounting problems.

These leaders are facing a management crisis. Often, the people who made an organization successful are not always able to keep up with the requirements of their jobs as both their company and the industry as a whole grow and become more complex. To deal with the problem of management obsolescence, companies must somehow integrate new and fresh perspectives into their organizations by attracting young engineering and scientific personnel while making sure that their more mature (or tenured) staff keep up to date in their fields and are contributing to the companies' performance.

Doing what others do in the area of compensation is turning out to be a waste of money. The companies with SPVCs generally have given up on this approach to compensation management. Every key leader of such companies is interested in learning how to improve corporate performance and how to use financial rewards better, and most want to escape the me-too approach to management compensation planning. All can cite situations where they believe their compensation programs have let them down. However, the executives are willing to experiment with something different in the management compensation area if they think their company can do better as a result of the change.

Job-Evaluation Practices

All organizations have some approach to the evaluation of management jobs and only a few of the smaller companies still try to pay the person rather than to pay the job. Those that pay the person believe that their companies are made up of individual performers whose jobs change so quickly that adopting a system using, for example, a maturity curve or market ranking is appropriate. In most instances, these organizations are in the group of companies with weak performance value cultures that advocate the recognition and rewarding of only individual performance. Although other companies used a philosophy of pay the person during their formative years, most eventually abandoned the approach because they found it too burdensome administratively once the companies grew beyond a few people and because it caused an excessive amount of distrust and confusion among employees.

Many high technology companies use some form of formal job evaluation system for management jobs. These systems fall into three general classifications: market ranking, point factor, and all other types. Although many systems use maturity curves at one time or another during their development, the use of curves generally is reserved for the evaluation of jobs below the management level. For the purposes of this book, *management job evaluation* means the formal evaluation of jobs in the top three to six levels of management in the company. *Evaluation* is the common yardstick developed to determine what a job is worth to the organization and to then reconcile this measurement with what the company believes the job is worth in the labor market.

Existing management compensation surveys are not providing key leaders with the information they need to make good compensation decisions. No exploration of job evaluation can be attempted without some discussion of the use of compensation surveys in the high technology industry because high technology companies are participants in compensation surveys of all sorts. Each company investigated for this book sponsored an average of 3.8 management compensation surveys of some type over the eighteen-month period prior to the investigation and participated in an average of 5.2 surveys over the same period. Some of the surveys were of a few management jobs and some were of all management jobs. The survey samples varied from large to small companies, and their designs varied from very sophisticated to very simple. Of the many types of surveys being conducted today, some are very good and some leave much to be desired.

Company personnel staff may conduct a survey or the company may hire consultants, as either part of a compensation project or on a regular basis, to conduct a survey. The survey data obtained by either method are confusing and results may be inconsistent. In some cases, a search company or employment agency conducts a survey of a single job the company is trying to fill; some of these surveys' data are of doubtful value. Most of the information obtained by surveys is about base salary and annual bonuses. Few surveys attempt to assign value to the total compensation managers receive from their jobs, and those that do are extremely costly.

Both widely held and closely held companies frequently are included in the same compensation survey. One executive interviewed for this book complained that his job was included in a survey of chief executives, even though he owns 25 percent of the common stock in his company. Because his job was in the survey, he did not find the survey's results credible.

All companies can use the reliable information that management compensation surveys provide, but few executives believe that most surveys provide accurate data about what other firms do. There certainly is a need for a good national survey of the high technology industry, but such a survey must explore the reasons for the existence of various compensation plans, not merely the compensation levels within companies.

Rank-to-Market Job Evaluation

Rank-to-market job evaluation often is the first system a company adopts. It also is used by companies that are seeking a more workable approach to job evaluation. The process of ranking to market does not tend to vary from organization to organization. Usually, the company relies heavily on one or two compensation surveys, although the survey sources may not be common.

To rank to market, a company compares its jobs with those in the compensation surveys and determines the extent to which the jobs are accurately matched. Companies use an average, median, or some other statistical reflection of the survey results to determine how jobs should be paid. In some cases, companies may do this only for base salaries; in other instances, companies may do this for both base salaries and annual incentive awards. Salary ranges generally have their midpoints placed at the market salary the company defines as competitive for the job.

Of the companies investigated for this book, about a quarter of them used market ranking for the evaluation of management jobs. Most of these companies performed less profitably than did the other high technology companies investigated. The reason most often cited for using this approach was the company's need to reflect the standards in the high technology labor market. A few of these market ranking organizations used other methods before trying market ranking; however, most of these companies have never used any other approach to evaluating management jobs.

Few SPVC companies use rank-to-market evaluation. It seems that, to communicate strong performance values effectively, companies need a better job evaluation method. Some of the more successful of these companies are seeking a progressive alternative to market ranking. The reason for the search is that, from an administrative standpoint, there are problems with the market ranking approach because the system communicates only the worth of jobs in the market, not the SPVs of the corporate culture. Market ranking SPVC companies have become frustrated with the inconsistent market information they obtain from the surveys, and some of the companies also are concerned about the appropriateness of the concept of comparable worth.

Some key leaders whose companies use market ranking view it as the best of what they feel are unsatisfactory alternatives for the evaluation of management jobs. Many view market ranking as good enough until something better comes along. Because of this, and the fact that successful SPVC companies tend not to use market ranking because it does not communicate the strong performance values that drive their cultures, the use of market ranking is likely to diminish as time goes by and other methods that add a formal internal measure to the determination of job worth are developed.

Point-Factor Job Evaluation

About half of the organizations that have formal job evaluation plans use some type of point-factor approach to evaluate management jobs. In addition, companies that perform well prefer point-factor to market ranking systems because it allows them to choose the compensable factors that communicate their SPVs. In this approach to job evaluation, management jobs usually are evaluated as part of a broader job evaluation study that includes most jobs in the company. The reasons for including senior jobs in the study are to help to communicate the reasons behind assigned job values and to add to the credibility of the program.

Point-factor plans use a series of compensable factors designed to measure elements of job worth, such as scope, in terms of the job's financial and nonfinancial responsibilities, its impact on the company performance (with regard to the importance of the decisions the incumbent can make), or the span of its accountability or authority (as measured by the number of people directed by the incumbent or the functional management responsibilities of the job). In companies with SPVCs, SPVs are used as compensable factors. The compensable factors are then assigned weights (or points) that total 100 percent of the job worth. The job with the most points is placed in the highest salary grade, and all other jobs are evaluated and placed in salary grades accordingly.

Some point-factor plans miss the essential compensable elements of management jobs. The most serious problem with point-factor plans is their inability to capture the specific and changing requirements of jobs in high technology companies. Some executives believe that the results of an internal valuing process cannot reflect the realities of the technical labor market. A number of companies use alternative salary ranges to ensure that the results of point-factor job evaluation does not place a job in a salary range that is comparable to those in the labor market. In several high technology companies, one set of salary ranges is used for technical managers and another is used for administrative managers. The use of alternatives may lead to credibility problems. Every time an organization has to add a few more points to make a job fit, acceptance of the results of the program will erode a bit more. The solution that will permit companies to use the program and also enable them to respond to changes in the labor market has yet to be found.

A number of executives feel that the compensable factors themselves do not reflect what makes managerial jobs valuable in a high technology organization. For example, management in a technically complex field frequently cannot be measured accurately by the number of people supervised, working conditions, or the internal and external contacts required by the job. These factors are not relevant to management jobs in a high technology company and, if they are used as compensable factors, the results of the point-factor evaluation are not likely to be credible.

Possible Job Evaluation Solutions

The leading companies in the high technology industry are trying to "fix" their evaluation programs. They are attempting to fine tune the plans so that they will work better or to apply logic to the point-factor plan to diffuse some of its variables. Very often, this fixing is viewed as a disruptive and time-consuming activity. And at the end of the repair work, many plans do not work any better; they still do not reflect the market, and they may have lost a great deal of their credibility.

The SPVC organizations that use point-factor plans both develop and repair the plans with better success than other high technology companies experience. This is because these companies ensure that the compensable factors reflect the SPVs and, as a result, link the program to the company's culture, making the job evaluation plan consistent with the communication of SPVs throughout the company.

Among the organizations investigated, those that preferred to use uniform systems to administer personnel practices were most satisfied with point-factor job evaluation plans, although they recognized that such plans, like any other administrative tool, communicate accurate messages only if they are attended to and kept current. Interestingly enough, these organizations had installed their programs within the past two or three years, so the programs were fairly fresh at the time of the investigation. The real problems seem to arise when such plans have been installed for several years and market circumstances have changed or when they have not been tended to since their installation. In these cases, managers are not always able to reconcile the internal value of a job with the dynamics of the market without tinkering with the job evaluation plan.

Those companies that expected the point-factor plan to resolve the problems they had in setting management base salaries without requiring maintenance attention are those that reported the most dissatisfaction with the program. Many of these firms tried to repair the plans by adding factors, changing factor weights, or installing alternative salary ranges for each technical and administrative area. These adjustments work only when the culture of the company was initially considered in the plan design. Companies with SPVCs tend to have the best success with point-factor plans because they ensure that the plans are linked to their SPVCs at the time of the plan development.

If an answer to the question of how to best design a job evaluation system is to be found, it probably will be found in a high technology company because of the industry's creativity and innovation. Already an entire category of other job evaluation systems exists in this industry. Covering the spectrum of alternatives that result from the companies' tinkering with existing programs, the category was referred to earlier as "everything else."

Companies that are not using pure market ranking or point-factor plans for one reason or another have devised approaches to job evaluation that combine facets of the disciplines of psychology and mathematics with a variety of other fields, including what some would call witchcraft or black magic. The best approaches reflect the culture of the company in every way possible. The most interesting of the alternatives are those that try to deal with what managers say they find objectionable about job evaluation. One attempt eliminates the formal position description, replacing it with either a questionnaire or a check list that can be used to determine the basic information about the management job and how it relates to the strong performance values. Another attempts to describe and set the salary range for each increasingly complex skill level while retaining the ability to adjust the final result to the market on an annual basis. This approach is intended to permit each technological area to respond to its market; in other words, it is trying to correlate the final results of job evaluation to more than one labor market. Yet another uses a series of compensable factors that reflect the SPVs but that can be adjusted as the content of a job changes. These compensable job factors describe the SPVs an individual has to learn and then sustain in order to progress up the career ladder within the job family.

For example, in addition to being phrased in a way that reflects the organization's SPVs, a compensable factor may identify a specific skill, such as microcircuit engineering, that spans as many as four or five job levels. As the job incumbent gains additional skills in this area, the compensable factor must be flexible enough to reflect that what the incumbent learns changes as the technology becomes more advanced. The use of standard phrases, then, is not always appropriate when creating such factors.

The need for careful definition of compensable factors is even more crucial for the evaluation of managerial jobs. Management in high technology companies, as in other industries, often is considered a separate skill from the technical skills of the individuals being managed. Key leaders view management as a series of job characteristics rather than as a single job element. Management at the highest level may be defined in terms of the incumbent's responsibility for directing a functional area, which, for the key leader, is the entire organization and, for top executives, is a specific operational area, such as sales, finance, or technology.

An obvious function of management is the direction of people. A compensable factor may differentiate the number of people being supervised from the complexity of the tasks the individuals being supervised perform. The number of people directed often is not an appropriate yardstick for measuring the worth of a technical manager's job; rather, it is the function the subordinates perform that is the crucial indicator of worth. For example, the supervision of clerical functions is assigned one specific worth, regardless of the number of people directed, and the supervision of research scientists, regardless of the number, is given a higher worth.

Above all, these evolving systems are flexible. In one instance, job characteristics, rather than specific jobs, may be assigned worth, so that responsibilities are valued first and then placed in management jobs. By avoiding the direct evaluation of each job, the approach is making sure that each job is evaluated fairly. In another instance, a wide range of technical, financial, sales, marketing, and other SPV components are described. Each SPV is assigned a dollar worth, with so many dollars assigned for one level of responsibility in sales management, so many dollars for a specific level of responsibility in business planning, and so on. Management jobs are granted the total number of dollars assigned to the SPV components that make up the job. The dollar worth of each SPV is changed each year to respond to the current market value of jobs that require the performance of these particular duties.

The companies that do not build the external market value into their plans determine, instead, the internal relationships between jobs. For example, a company may use the job evaluation system to establish the internal relationships between management jobs. Then, after this is accomplished, the internal ranking is compared to the market and the jobs are placed in the salary ranges that best fit the external labor market. The resultant salary ranges are not very neat, but they are very functional.

In conclusion, given the realities of directing a high technology company, the rapid changes in job content, and the dynamics of the market for management personnel, established job evaluation systems are proving ineffective for management positions in high technology. Although many companies still use pure market ranking and point-factor plans, more and more of them are finding that such plans do not work well. The companies that are accustomed to administrative regimentation are the ones most satisfied with point-factor plans. However, as companies must become more flexible in response to the ever-changing business conditions, so must their compensation plans become more pliable.

High technology tinkerers are working to improve their plans. The most successful companies use SPVs as compensable factors. These firms have set out to design plans that are more responsive to their needs. Their solutions are offering different directions from the general trend in management job evaluation. Some plans are hybrids of historical solutions, while others break all the rules of traditional job evaluation and attempt new solutions. The plans that give the best results diagnose the corporate culture and design a job evaluation method that matches the culture.

Incentive-Plan Practices

Incentives often are the key to getting a failing organization going again. Incentives must communicate and reward behavior that is consistent with the company's SPVs. They should communicate the SPVs throughout the organization in a consistent manner that shows managers how to produce profit in a culturally appropriate manner.

The companies with strong performance value cultures have an acknowledged way of conducting business, relating to people, and solving problems. Their administrative systems are designed to match the cultures that support them. For example, their business strategies and tactics reflect their SPVs, and budgets are handled and money is accounted for in ways that are consistent with the companies' cultural values. In those companies, the working relationships between supervisors and subordinates are predictable because they are determined by the strong performance value cultures of the organizations and are communicated by informal communication networks that reinforce the companies' particular strong performance values. The specific values may relate to technical excellence, performance through cooperative effort, or a similar goal. All the values clearly indicate the way employees should make money for their companies. Those employees who consistently perform in step with the SPVC are rewarded financially and thus are given the incentive to continue to perform in step.

Incentives and Culture

The need for the effective communication of cultural objectives is the best reason for developing an incentive plan. The incentive plans in companies with SPVCs follow the formal and informal communications channels and reward the behavior that the culture deems valuable. The culture provides guidance about how managers should behave, and incentive plans reward this behavior. Incentive plans, like other compensation plans, should be designed to be flexible and permit the manager to alter performance criteria in response to a change in the business or technical environment.

For example, in most companies, managers must make choices that can have a substantial impact on a business strategy or tactical plan. Often, a management incentive plan is tied to such strategies. In the companies with SPVCs, making corrective changes to strategies on the basis of new information or the reanalysis of existing data does not involve managers' choosing between working for the good of the company and working for a financial award. The SPVs and the incentive plans are well integrated; the incentive plans change in response to the dynamics of the business so that a reward always communicates the job to be performed.

Culture plays a major role in determining which managers will be groomed for leadership positions. Although one may argue with the idea that people work harder when they have a chance to earn more money, the idea that money can be used to communicate a message to people cannot be disputed. And when strong performance values are closely linked with financial incentives, the incentives themselves can communicate important behaviors and goals. Managers learn, through the awarding of incentives, what the key leader believes they should do in order to earn promotions. The key leader will look for management behavior that will perpetuate his or her strong performance values and will reward such behavior accordingly. Managers may seek incentive rewards, then, as much for what they mean in terms of professional growth as for their financial worth.

One problem in the high technology industry is that professionals tend to associate themselves more strongly with their professions than they do with their employers. In addition, technical management skills can be transferred easily between high technology companies. Thus, to earn the loyalty and trust of their employees, companies use incentive plans, linked with

SPVs, that develop greater company loyalty than professional loyalty among managers.

Incentives and Performance

The rewarding of individual performance can be a frustrating area of management compensation. Many managers complain about how difficult it can be to grant financial rewards that are consistent with the contributions of the individual. Because of the industry's emphasis on teamwork, attributing contributions to individuals can lead to internal competition or strife and poor, rather than improved, performance. The rewarding of group incentives are a solution to this problem.

Although they all understand the importance of individual performance, key leaders of companies with SPVCs believe that the best interests of the company can be attained by identifying similar work goals for smaller work groups and by channeling the groups' efforts through the use of incentive plans that reward cooperative behavior and teamwork. Reward programs that reward cooperative performance often cut across organizational lines and disciplines. When meeting a specific market need or improving a technology cannot be done effectively by a single individual, smaller units, often with members from dissimilar disciplines, must be formed to solve the problem or meet the need. Such work units often are tied together by a financial reward system and strong performance values that guide the groups' efforts toward a specific, defined result.

Most high technology companies' management incentive plans are based on the net profit performance of the company over a twelve-month period. Most of these plans call for the awarding of incentives at the end of the year or performance period. The average annual incentive award for the performance period prior to the time the research for this book was conducted was approximately 22 percent of a manager's base salary. Although some ''zero'' awards were granted, the number was not substantial, except in many of the companies with strong performance value cultures. This finding suggests that the concept of awarding individual performance, as advocated by many companies with weak and mixed performance value cultures, is not well practiced. If it were, more zero incentive awards would be given in those companies, which are, after all, achieving less than exceptional overall results. The high technology companies that grant more zero awards to those managers and members of work groups who do not meet their performance goals are communicating a credible message about pay for performance. Financial rewards are more meaningful in these companies because they reflect performance differences. This may be one reason why these companies are doing better financially.

When incentive awards are given on the basis of group performance, more qualitative criteria must be used to measure performance. Present incentive plan performance criteria are not related to the overall performance of a work group or organizational unit. Criteria that measure improvement in qualitative performance from year to year need to be identified. Key leaders are interested in sustaining performance and, in many cases, want to find a way to integrate short-term incentive plans with the methods they use to reward long-term performance.

Many of SPVC companies are designing unique incentive plans. Much of their work is aimed at including qualitative performance criteria for determining award amounts. The companies also are working on linking their SPVs more closely with their incentive plans. Such plans emphasize one or more basic corporate performance value, and none focuses only on the financial performance of the company or an organizational unit. The programs establish both quantitative and qualitative milestones. For example, technical excellence cannot be measured in quantitative terms. Gaining a technical advantage involves more than a year's work in most instances, and scientific or technical performance can be recognized only indirectly or after an extended period of time through the use of financial measures.

Incentives and Recognition

The SPVC companies that perform the best financially tend to use special award programs to recognize achievements because the financial impact of a technological breakthrough may not be reflected on the corporate balance sheet for years. Managements in the companies with SPVCs want to reinforce good business and technical performance incrementally as soon as possible after the work is done. Because top executives want managers to understand that the business and technical foundation of the company is based on gaining and then keeping a competitive advantage, they want to communicate the importance of business and technical strength constantly. An incentive plan that is based on the current year's profit performance may be rewarding innovations or strategies that evolved a number of years ago. Managers will continue their search for technical breakthroughs or good business results if their successes are rewarded and reinforced more frequently. Hence, a need exists for some kind of award program that reinforces performance.

Various special award programs help to meet this need for performance reinforcement. In many companies, a short ceremony is held each month. In a brief meeting held during regular working hours, the key leader announces the contribution of an individual or group of individuals and makes the award (usually checks) on the spot. In most instances, these awards are given for some progress that was made toward a longer-term qualitative goal. Awards are made for incremental achievements as well as for the end results.

Managers who receive this sort of recognition for work well done are acknowledged by their key leader and by their peers as well as rewarded financially. The meetings serve not only to recognize good performance but also to indicate to other employees what they must do to earn rewards. The meetings teach managers that performing in accord with the company's strong performance values is worthwhile to them, both financially and in terms of peer and upper management recognition.

Formal incentive plans also may include qualitative criteria. In many instances, incentive plans include written descriptions of the type of performance that is desirable. Performance standards are expressed in broad terms that communicate the strong performance values of the organization but permit interpretation according to the needs of each business or technical situation. Confusion and inaccurate expectations are handled through the actual face-to-face administration of the plan. An award is granted and strokes are given with a specific oral and written description of the reason for the award, how the accomplishment being awarded fits in with the long- and short-term objectives of the work unit or company, and expectations for continuing progress. In this way, the company's long- and short-term objectives are reinforced for both the recipient of the award and his or her co-workers.

Organizations that combine qualitative and quantitative performance criteria in special award programs and formal incentive plans report that they get more from these programs, despite the extra effort their administration requires, than they got when they granted only larger awards on the basis of financial criteria.

Good incentive plans are never finalized. They always can be improved upon. Plans must have maximum flexibility; an award's message should be based upon the specific role the individual or group plays within the company—it should not be a standard, or canned, recognition. The managers who have participated in these flexible programs report that special awards make them feel more like entrepreneurs than employees. They like the idea that they can get an award at any time during the year, and they appreciate that the plan means there is no particular time of year when performance will influence judgments about who will receive an award.

As they are doing with job evaluation plans, many SPVC companies are creating their own incentive plans to match the cultures of their organizations. These companies seem to be less concerned about what others are doing; instead, they are directing their efforts toward communicating their primary strong performance values. They believe that the best way to get the most mileage out of their management incentive/compensation dollars is to reinforce relevant group goals through financial rewards.

They use the incentive plan awards as levers to move the organizations in the direction its key leaders want them to go.

In response to being described as a tinkerer, an executive interviewed during the research said, "Tinkering and innovation are bedfellows in high technology organizations. If we don't tinker with something someone else has designed, we will continue to repeat his errors or, at best, be a follower to his lead." When asked about the administrative burden that such a process seemed to create, he said, "We want to look for the simple solution to a problem. If we find that the simple solution does not work, we adopt something more complicated that does work, get some experience with it, and then see if we can simplify it." In the high technology industry, where innovation is a way of life, when a traditional approach does not work, it is adjusted or rebuilt. This is the way SPVC companies have approached incentive plans.

Short-Term Incentive Plans

All of the organizations investigated for this book used short-term incentive plans for managers. A short-term plan awards payment at the end of a period of twelve months or less. Monetary awards are granted separately from adjustments to base salary. In the companies investigated, management jobs at four to six levels down from the chief executive and, in some cases, senior nonmanagement jobs were defined as the lowest level of jobs qualified to be part of management incentive plans. Plans that extended below the management level were included in the investigation because a large number of the high technology companies use annual incentive plans throughout their organizations.

Approximately half of the executives interviewed stated that they did not completely like the way their companies' incentive plans worked and they were less than fully satisfied with their short-term plans. Most were dissatisfied with the performance criteria used; many of the key leaders believed that some measures of performance in addition to financial ones should be used.

Because of this dissatisfaction, many companies are changing their plans. About two-thirds of the organizations investigated had changed the basic design of their short-term incentive plans within the previous twenty-four months. Although many executives admitted that one reason they changed their companies' plans was that awards were not being made, even though the company was performing well, the principal reason they gave for making the change was that they believed that the original plan had not been flexible enough to respond to changes in their companies business situations. A number of key leaders were concerned about whether the short-term incentive plans were really helping their organizations. They reported confusion about the awarding of incentives, which they attributed to the plans. In some cases, they were concerned that their plans either paid more employees than they felt should be awarded or failed to reward enough contributions because the rules were too rigid.

Short-term incentive plans that use only financial criteria do not work well because, as was stated earlier, not all performance results in something that can be measured in financial terms. Using both financial and nonquantitative criteria ensures that all contributions will be rewarded.

A typical short-term incentive plan in high technology companies utilizes a pool of incentive dollars that is distributed at the end of a fiscal year on the basis of some measure of performance, rather than a specific financial target. The size of the pool depends on the company's net profit improvement, adjusted for any inflationary impact of a sales increase. Some form of management by objectives or a formula relating to job level, salary grade, or the base salary of the individual at the time of the award are common yardsticks for determining how the pool will be distributed among employees.

Companies with mixed and weak performance value cultures often design their short-term incentive plans separately from other administrative systems and, perhaps, too hurriedly. In many of these companies, plan design is delegated to one financial or personnel executive, and the key leader and other executives review the plan only after much of the work on it has been completed. The top executives' role is limited to review and approval rather than active participation in designing the plan. Because such companies do not want to expend much time or effort in creating short-term plans, their plans often are copies of plans used by their large and successful competitors. Some of the executives interviewed admitted that they selected their specific plan designs because they were similar to plans the executives knew had worked elsewhere or because the plans were shown to be popular in a compensation survey.

Long-Term Incentive Plans

A long-term incentive plan grants awards based on performance over a period of time longer than a year. It is intended to reward sustained performance that is consistent with the goals and objectives of the company. Stock options are very popular forms of long-term incentives. All but the privately held high technology companies use stock option plans as the principal form of long-term incentive. A review of the growth in the market value of stock in these companies over the last few years indicates that the value of common stock has appreciated—more so than might be expected of the high technology industry in general.

Key leaders who originally were either corporate founders or principal technical contributors at the time of the organization's establishment often still have stock options. Most hold a large portion of the company's common stock as the result of either receiving direct stock grants or their exercising their prior stock options. Because these key leaders hold a large proportion of their companies stock, they believe in the worth of stock as a reward. Even if the key leader does not have a substantial equity position in the company but is interested in obtaining one, he or she may have a bias toward the granting of common stock to acquire and reward managers.

High technology organizations tend to have some association with venture capital suppliers at one time or another during their development. Venture capitalists provided the original leadership for some companies. In a number of the established firms, venture capitalists still play some role in at least the indirect management of the companies. They often are represented on the board of directors, and they frequently serve on the chairman of the board's compensation committee. These individuals often participate in the designing of long-term incentive plans that involve the granting of company stock.

The objective of the venture capitalists is to increase the worth of the company to its shareholders. This objective is dominant in all companies where these individuals are present. They are concerned about the possible dilution of equity ownership, and they prefer that financial criteria, ones popular in the financial community or ones that indicate to potential merger or acquisition suiters how the company is doing, be used to measure performance. The venture capitalists' influence on the use of long-term incentives, particularly those that involve company stock, can be an important determinant of incentive plan design.

Managers want a piece of the high technology pie; they want to be more than just employees. Thus, whether direct stock awards, restricted stock, or stock options should be used is a question that permeates all discussions about long-term incentive plan designs. Key leaders, and nearly all managers, believe that the ability to award managers a piece of the pie gives a company an advantage over their high technology competitors. On average, nearly 11 percent of the total common stock outstanding was held either directly or at option by the incumbents of management jobs in the top four levels of the high technology companies that participated in the research for this book. In many instances, when the top managers were members of their companies' boards of directors, they said that they must directly associate their financial interests with those of public shareholders. In other words, many high technology companies are led by owner-managers who have a stake in the success of the enterprise.

About half of the companies investigated used incentive stock options (ISOs), many having converted to their use recently. The reason given for conversion was the tax advantages of these programs to the recipients of the ISOs. Among the companies that did not use incentive stock options at the time of investigation, most were considering them. In many of the companies that used stock and stock options, the daily stock price was posted so that managers would be aware of the price of their company's stock. These companies emphasized that managers would increase the price of their stock by performing well.

Linking the manager with the financial fortunes of the company is considered essential to sustained corporate profit performance. This view of the importance of long-term incentive plans does not vary among executives; key leaders of companies with SPVCs and those of companies with MPVCs and WPVCs have similar views of existing plans. The concept of sharing the stock in the organization, however, is not so universally approved. The companies with strong performance value cultures—the best corporate performers—are much more willing to distribute the ownership of their companies. The key leaders of these firms want more people to share in the action because they feel this is a good way to engender management team work. These top executives believe that awarding common stock is an important way of gaining managers' long-term commitment to the performance objectives of their organizations. They feel that managers will identify with the overall performance values of the company better if they own stock.

Each of these key leaders has an approach to the distribution of stock or stock options that seems to be fairly consistent with his or her management style. In many instances, stock options are granted annually without a formula or formal plan. The chief executive makes allocations subject to the approval of the board of directors. In only a few cases is a strict, formal policy used to determine the specific number of options that are to be granted.

Long-term incentive plans that are paid out in cash rather than common stock or some other asset generally apply to a limited number of top managers, more limited than the number of managers who participate in the stock plans. The nonstock plans used most often fall into the categories of performance share, performance unit or sequential bonus award, which will be discussed later in this book. The measure of performance most commonly used is improvement in corporate earnings per share, although other criteria, including corporate cash-flow improvement, net profit performance, and growth in sales, also are used. These plans usually supplement rather than replace the popular stock option plans. Although projections of the financial worth of nonstock incentive plans are not always accurate, the companies interviewed that used these long-term plans estimated that the plans provided about 15 to 20 percent of the total compensation for their management group. If linked with SPVs, then, these plans can be worthwhile and important communicators of preferred managerial behavior.

A pressing concern of senior high technology executives is whether the growth in stock prices experienced over the last few years can be sustained.

Although the key leaders believe that managers who share in the financial success of the company help keep the excitement of an entrepreneurial environment alive, they are concerned about whether stock options being granted now will offer their managers the opportunity to build an estate. Executives view their stock price as fairly fragile because their industry is so dependent on innovation. They are looking for ways to stabilize long-term financial rewards so they can ensure the retention of their most valuable managers.

Top executives of companies that use incentive compensation plans in addition to ISOs believe that younger managers feel that the rewards non-stock plans provide are too far in the future. The executives are worried that ISOs do not provide sufficient immediate reward. Even though the price of their common stock has increased over the last few years and their companies' performance is projected to improve over the next few years, the leaders feel the increases in stock prices may not keep up with how well their companies are doing and thus may not continue to respond to the expectations of their managers. However, many of these leaders feel that internal financial measures may not accurately reflect the true value of their managers' contributions, either. Thus, over half of the key leaders interviewed were seeking supplements to stock options.

In addition to providing sufficient reward to current managers, executives want to be able to dislodge key individuals from other companies who are locked in their present jobs because of the holding period and appreciation in their current stock option plans. The something in addition to common stock and stock options, then, should provide a progressive solution to all reward problems.

The problems created by the potential dilution of equity ownership and the executives' uncertainty about the future growth in the price of their stocks has resulted in more high technology tinkering with incentive plans. The thrust of such tinkering in the SPVC companies is in tying the long-term incentive plans to the strong performance values. Few of these companies challenge the importance or relevance of increases in the price of stock as a measure of the success of the company and as an important incentive for continued success. They are concerned, however, about the managers who do not have an equity position in their companies. Because executives believe that newer managers may not be able to obtain a meaningful stock position, they fear that such managers may not associate their interests to those of the company as strongly as owner-managers do. In addition, key leaders of SPVC companies often consider that measuring performance by improvement in the price of their common stock is too remote a measurement—it does not serve to reinforce their most important SPVs. The price of the common stock is a delayed measure of the performance of the company. By the time a significant contribution is reflected in improvements in the worth of the company to its shareholders, the association between the reward and the contribution that earned the reward may be lessened. The executives want additional rewards that are more closely tied in time to the contributions.

Strong performance values, such as relationships to competitors, response to customers and the business environment, and technical excellence, are not directly reflected in the price of stock or in any financial measure of corporate performance. To communicate to management the importance of these SPVs, executives need to reward behavior that is consistent with them in a symbolic manner or financially through short-term incentive plans. In addition, they need to reward such behavior with their long-term incentive plan, and this will require most firms to adjust, or tinker with, their long-term plans.

Possible Incentive Plan Solutions

Companies with strong performance value cultures are not the only companies concerned about the effectiveness of their long-term incentive plans. All companies seem to want something more than financially driven long-term incentive plans. Thus, much work is being done on incentive plans, and it does not seem to be the result of any visible exchange of information. The common dissatisfaction with present programs results from internal pressures. Of the sixty-six organizations included in the research for this book, twenty-four were at some stage of a search for a supplement to their stock option programs, many of them with outside assistance. Very few of the SPVC companies, however, have delegated the design projects totally to an external resource, however, because they have identified the work in this area as an urgent priority.

The companies involved in redesigning their incentive plans are doing so in various ways. The directions being followed are not completely consistent between organizations. However, much of the work focuses on defining, in clearer terms, what the companies want their managers to do to obtain financial rewards. For example, a number of SPVC companies have linked their short-term incentive plans to their long-term plans by defining accomplishments made within the year as milestones toward the final long-term result. The achievement of qualitative SPV objectives, then, are rewarded not only by the short-term plan but also by the long-term plan.

Many SPVC companies are looking long and hard at restricted stock plans (and at so-called junior stock plans). These plans define requirements, or restrictions, that must be satisfied before ownership of the asset, usually common stock, is transferred to the employee. These requirements usually are financial in nature, but the SPVC organizations are redefining the restrictions in terms of the qualitative and quantitative requirements for a reward under their short-term plans. In this way, too, they are able to link qualitative and quantitative SPVs to both long- and short-term plans.

Associating SPVs to restricted stock plans will be particularly valuable in identifying nonquantitative milestones that reinforce the SPVs of the organization, in sustaining the communication process of SPVs throughout the organization, and in associating the total financial reward system with the SPVC of the company. If incentive plans of this type are implemented in companies with weak or mixed performance value cultures, they not only will provide supplements to stock option plans but also will help the organizations establish strong performance values because the plans themselves will serve as means of communication.

A number of the most profitable companies are investigating long-term plans that do not use financial criteria at all. Used in combination with ISO plans, these nonfinancial long-term incentive plans generally define the areas in which a group of individuals should concentrate its efforts, such as engineering, sales, market research, or personnel relations. Accomplishments in these areas are related to the achievement of the SPVs of the company. To administer these plans, representatives of long-term incentive-compensation committees meet with team members to review progress, establish SPV milestones, and discuss the relationship of their work to the work of others in the company, thereby reinforcing overall corporate objectives. The committee makes periodic financial awards to members of each team for milestones accomplished along the way. The grants are paid in cash or stock at the election of the employee. Award funds also may be invested in the undertaking. The funds, plus appreciation, are then granted at the end of the performance period—usually three years.

Effective management of the human assets of a company is the most important contributor to profitable end results. Managers are responsible for creating an environment in which employees have the best opportunity to make important contributions, and they are the link between the key leaders and employees. Although this may hold true for all companies, in a high technology organization, the role the manager plays may be one of the most important roles in the company because the industry is labor intensive. It takes a lot of time and effort to bring a manager, whether scientist, engineer, or nontechnical, to the point where he or she buys on to the corporate culture and to what the organization is trying to do. Incentive plans that ensure low voluntary turnover rates and a stable, high quality work force are essential administrative tools in this area.

Supplemental Management Compensation

Management benefits and perquisites do not help a company do better financially, but poor benefits plans can be costly. In the research for this book, investigators studied the extent to which managers in the top four to six levels of the organization received noncash compensation in addition to the benefits and perquisites offered to the employee population in general. The principal areas of interest were additional retirement benefits, death benefits, medical benefits, use of company automobiles, or optional benefits or perquisites to be selected by each individual.

Most of the companies investigated offered extra benefits and perquisites to top managers. The culture of the organization did not have much to do with the type of benefits offered. However, small organizations tended both to offer more liberal extra benefits and perquisites and to offer them to lower management ranks than did the larger companies.

In the companies with SPVCs, executives preferred to concentrate money on salaries and incentives. They viewed extra benefits and perquisites principally from the standpoint of tax consequences. Although few believed that benefits and perquisites contributed to company performance, many believed that they were a potential source of discontent among employees. Top executives find it very difficult to develop and administer rules concerning who will receive extra compensation. Organizations that have the most liberal management benefits and perquisites often are those that view them as more of a nuisance than an advantage.

The few organizations that treat all employees similarly from a benefits standpoint and do not offer extra noncash compensation to any employees can run into some trouble when they want to hire top managers from outside the organization. The individuals they want to hire may be accustomed to such extras as the use of company automobiles and membership in a country club. If the companies offer these compensation forms to attract managers from outside the company, this will disrupt what the organizations' key leaders view as an important internal cultural characteristic—similar benefits for everyone.

A number of top executives believe that they must offer perquisites and extra management benefits because the community of high technology managers is such a homogenous one that employees are more apt to move to an organization that offers a compensation advantage, even if the move would involve their leaving a culture that is particularly productive.

Because key leaders in companies with SPVCs prefer to take an offensive position when it comes to management compensation, it is no surprise that they do not see much value in benefits and perquisites which they classify as defensive forms of management compensation. There is very little tinkering with management benefits and perquisites. Key leaders see too great an opportunity in improving the areas of salary administration and incentive/compensation plans to direct their efforts to management benefits and perquisites. The one development in the benefit and perquisite area that some executives see as important is the concept of variable benefits. This new development in the compensation area, which allows managers to choose among benefits offered, provides a long-range opportunity for meeting employee needs while containing benefit costs.

Key leaders in the best companies are most interested in obtaining an advantage from the dollars they spend on management compensation. They want the compensation they offer to reinforce their organizations' SPVCs, and they do not see benefits and perquisites as relevant to the communication of SPVs. However, they do see variable benefits as a cost containment opportunity. One executive interviewed in the study responded to questions about liberalizing management benefits and perquisites as follows: "When we are in such a strong market position that I can give my managers the time to use the extra benefits, I will liberalize management benefits. Right now, I am looking for a way to get people to work smarter. I do not see how giving someone a country club membership can help me do this. I do see an advantage in working to get more than we do out of the incentive dollars we spend, and I want to emphasize this area. However, giving people choices makes good sense because we can give people what they really want and still control costs. Variable benefits are on the way."

Summary

The SPVC companies are moving toward the use of management compensation programs that help to reinforce their successful cultures, including formal job evaluation programs that evaluate jobs with the use of compensable factors that communicate strong performance values. In the incentive area, top managements are looking for opportunities to use both qualitative and quantitative measures of management success and to integrate short- and long-term incentive plans in rewarding performance that is consistent with their organizations' SPVCs. Executives are enthusiastic about the use of variable benefits as replacement for liberal perquisites and benefits plans that can respond to employee preferences and still contain costs.

4 Management Job-Evaluation Methods

High technology companies have a number of good alternatives from which to choose when selecting a way to establish the worth of management jobs. The high technology tinkerers may use these alternatives as the bases for developing the approach that best communicates their most important strong performance values.

One method is based on the market value of management jobs—market ranking; another uses comparable elements to establish the worth of jobs in quantitative terms—point factor. These methods were discussed briefly in chapter 3. In this chapter, they will be discussed in more detail, along with a technique that reflects the comparable elements that make jobs more or less valuable to the company in qualitative terms—knowledge and abilities. All three approaches work well; however, depending on the needs of individual organizations, one approach might look better than another. These are standard methods, and their adaptability to the special needs in high technology companies is another consideration that will be discussed here.

Management Job Evaluation

Many high technology companies have formal job evaluation programs. The programs enable the companies to design their communications on the foundation of the common understanding of the worth of each job. The best corporate performers use programs that measure the value of management jobs according to compensable elements. These elements (or factors) identify the structure or composition of each management job. In companies with SPVCs, the compensable factors reflect the organizations' strong performance values. The elements that are based on SPVs communicate to the managers what essential areas of performance are emphasized in their jobs. Job evaluation, then, is more than just a way to determine competitive salaries; it also is a communications route.

How the relative worth of jobs is determined in a company is an old and fundamental issue. A successful job evaluation plan establishes a hierarchy in which the jobs that are more important to the company are assigned a higher value, in terms of financial worth, than are jobs that are less important to the firm. Hopefully, this hierarchy will be credible to the incumbents of the jobs and will reflect the realities of the external market place. Thus, job evaluation reconciles each job's contribution to the company with its market worth and places the job within an equitable and credible salary range. Although computer technology has accelerated the job evaluation process and made it less cumbersome administratively, the basic principles underlying the process have not changed substantially since the early 1950s, despite the ongoing search for the ultimate job evaluation methodology. The steps followed to select a job evaluation system, describe jobs, gather market information, evaluate the jobs, and assign them to an appropriate dollar value remain fairly standard. However, it is important to understand this process if one is to improve it through the use of strong performance values.

Job Analysis

Jobs are studied in order to identify the duties and responsibilities that must be fulfilled for the successful performance of each job. Job analysis determines what must be done to perform a job, why it must be done, and how it is to be done. Job analysis provides a company with an explanation of the elements of its existing jobs, which gives top management a basis for deciding each job's relative worth. The first step in job analysis is defining and describing the jobs—in other words, the development of job information. This may entail the preparation of formal job descriptions and documentation of the essential duties and responsibilities of all of the jobs to be included in the job evaluation program.

In the early years of job evaluation, much time and effort was expended on the description of jobs and on the analysis of their contents. Although this can be a burdensome task, in a company that has fairly stable jobs, it seems to still be worthwhile, because it documents the basic building blocks of the company's various functional operations. In high technology companies, however, jobs change a great deal, making job descriptions obsolete so quickly that the long-term benefits of preparing job descriptions and conducting analyses are seldom realized. Those assigned the responsibility for job evaluation may become frustrated in their labors.

In a high technology company, then, the preparation of formal management job descriptions may stifle the organization by introducing a rigidity that is foreign to the company's culture. A popular alternative to formal evaluation is the use of position questionnaires. Administering these questionnaires makes it possible for the company to obtain the information it needs to perform job analysis without expending the time and energy preparing formal job descriptions requires.

Job Documentation

There are three ways to obtain job information: observation of what the manager does; interviews with the manager and his or her superior and subordinates; and the evaluation of a questionnaire prepared by the incumbent of the job and reviewed by his or her superior. Observing a busy manager to determine what he or she does is not a very practical alternative in a high technology company. Having someone trailing the manager and taking notes on what he or she does not only is potentially disruptive but probably will not yield insight into the job because some of the most important duties of a high technology manager may be performed infrequently.

Management interviews can be productive in high technology companies, providing the information needed within a reasonable period of time. As a result, interviews are a popular way of obtaining management job information. For the interview to be successful, it should be conducted by an interviewer who knows about high technology management jobs specifically and how high technology companies are managed in general. In a limited period of time, the interviewer must obtain the needed information, write up the results of the interview in the form of a job description, and review the description with the job incumbent and his or her immediate supervisor. Without the essential background information, no interviewer could provide accurate job information.

In recent years, the use of job questionnaires to obtain information on management jobs has become popular. Questionnaires have two important qualities: they do not have to be prepared in the form of a formal description to be completed by the manager and reviewed by his or her supervisor and/or they can be utilized in the job evaluation process without ever being prepared as a formal job description. Unless the company has some use for formal job descriptions besides job evaluation, a well-completed job questionnaire that provides all the necessary information can serve in place of a formal description. A third quality of management job questionnaires is that, as the jobs change, the questionnaires can be updated more easily than can formal job descriptions.

Although companies usually have some idea of which job evaluation approach they will be using before they obtain job information, the selection of a job evaluation method may be made after job information is gathered. One reason to defer the selection of a job evaluation approach is that accurate job information may provide a better basis on which to make the choice. When they know what their companies' management jobs require, key leaders may be able to make a more educated decision regarding the approach to use to organize that information. All methods of job evaluation require an understanding of the jobs to be evaluated and the gathering of job information may be the best means of gaining that understanding.

In some cases, the job documentation process itself determines whether the company will proceed with management job evaluation. If managers struggle and fumble with the job documentation process, or if the process yields meager results or causes considerable organizational strife, it probably is best to defer administering any job evaluation program until the organizational issues uncovered by the documentation of jobs are addressed and reconciled.

Job Evaluation Considerations

No one approach to management job evaluation is appropriate for all companies. The performance values and culture of an organization will determine which approach will provide the desired results. However, some evaluative criteria should be established to assist executives in the selection of a program that best meets their company's needs. Key leaders must have a basis and a justification for their choice of job evaluation. The criteria top management should consider in evaluating each job evaluation method are:

1. How precise is the method? Does it deal with the determination of job value in general or specific terms? Will it reflect the company's strong performance values?
2. Will the approach be credible to managers? Will managers believe that the method will create a job structure fairly and equitably?
3. Will the approach be able to respond to the changing needs of the organization and appropriately modify management jobs as the company grows? How easy will it be to integrate new and changing management jobs into the system?
4. Will the system created by this method be adaptable to changes in the structure of the company? Will the terminology of the job evaluation plan become obsolete over time?
5. Is the approach too complex to administer on a continuing basis? Can existing internal staff maintain the program in the future or will outside assistance be needed to keep the program working?
6. How does the method account for both the internal and external worth of a job? Will it account for rapid changes in the technical management labor market without losing its credibility?
7. Will the approach be easy to communicate to the managers whose jobs will be evaluated by the program? Is the approach's methodology clear and reasonable?
8. Can the company's human resource managers use the results for any other purpose? For example, can any of the information that is uncovered by the job evaluation process be used in performance appraisal, the development of career paths, or skills inventories?

Each of the methods discussed in this chapter will be evaluated on the basis of these considerations and whether it helps to strengthen a company's strong performance values. The experience high technology companies have had with the method also will be reviewed.

Compensation Surveys

What the industry needs is a single, accurate, up-to-date source of information on compensation levels for management personnel. Because job content varies widely and the structure of an organization seldom is fixed for a long period of time, it is not likely that one best survey that satisfies the diverse needs of even a significant proportion of its potential users will surface in the near future. Until it does, companies must sponsor and participate in a number of surveys on a periodic basis to get the management pay information they need.

A high technology company usually relies on a survey of benchmark jobs to obtain the information it needs to establish management salary ranges that are competitive in the market place. Benchmarks are those management jobs that are most likely to exist in all the organizations selected for the survey. Benchmark jobs must reflect the industry's most important disciplines, including engineering, marketing and sales, manufacturing, and distribution. In addition, a sample of jobs that may be comparable outside the high technology industry, such as personnel, procurement, and finance, should be included in the survey.

The benchmark jobs are used to design the survey. It is crucial, especially if job titles differ greatly, that the survey accurately compares the content of the jobs. A group of companies that are direct labor market and business competitors must be identified and a continuing information exchange with them must be established to ensure that the survey sample does not change from year to year. To ascertain the essential information about how the companies are organized and how their jobs compare most likely will require the representatives of the survey companies who know the jobs well to meet annually with the managers of the sample companies. In addition, it is important that the representatives find out the source of any drastic changes in reported compensation levels—whether due to changes in incumbents, changes in job duties, extraordinary compensation awards, or the like.

Once the survey information on the benchmark jobs has been obtained, these jobs should be the first to be evaluated under the job evaluation program selected. This will let top management know how well the job evaluation plan is working before they attempt to apply it to all management jobs in the company. In other words, the first test of the job evaluation plan is to determine how well it evaluates the key jobs on which external survey information is available.

Rank-to-Market Job Evaluation

The rank-to-market method does just what its name suggests. Jobs are ranked from highest to lowest based on their worth as determined by the results of the survey of benchmark jobs. The companies that have the most success with this method do not short cut the job information process. Documentation of individual jobs and of the management job market is essential to market ranking because the rank-to-market system uses whole job ranking. That is, each job is ranked as a total entity and is not broken down into its compensable elements, as it is with other job evaluation techniques.

Steps in Rank-to-Market Job Evaluation

The first step in rank-to-market job evaluation is selecting salary grades and ranges. The salary range midpoints should start about 20 percent below the survey weighted average of the lowest paid management job in the benchmark survey. The highest salary in the range should be about 25 percent above the highest job in the survey, assuming the highest job is within one organization level below the chief executive. This provides enough room to rank jobs in order of internal as well as market worth. In high technology companies, salary range midpoints usually are about 5 to 7 percent apart. Anything less makes it difficult to identify differences in job worth. If ranges are too close together for administrative purposes, unused grades may be omitted later.

The second step in this approach is ranking the benchmark jobs into the salary range having a midpoint that most closely approximates the company's objectives. For example, organizations that plan to pay base salaries that are somewhere near the simple or weighted average of the current market salary range place the jobs in grades having a midpoint that is as close as possible to the rate paid for the job in the market. In a number of instances, more sophisticated market definitions are made. Some companies define what the salary range midpoint means to them in terms of the administration of individual salaries. As a result, these companies may place the job in a salary range that is near the sixtieth or ninetieth percentile of the market range. Others may place the midpoint somewhere below the fiftieth percentile if they intend to leverage their total cash compensation toward incentive compensation.

A useful aid in the job ranking process is either a felt or magnet board. Titles of the management jobs can be written on tags that can be moved around the board by the individuals who are responsible for the job ranking process. This makes it easier to integrate new jobs into the plan and also makes job evaluation more of a management game for the job rankers.

The last step of this process is ranking the non-benchmark jobs within the salary structure. These management jobs are the ones on which market information is either not available or has not been obtained. These jobs may be peculiar to the specific company doing the ranking. Placing these jobs in pay grades is accomplished on a whole-job-ranking basis by comparing the jobs to the already ranked benchmark jobs. Jobs that are viewed as more important than the benchmark jobs are placed in a higher job grade, and jobs that are seen as less important are placed in a lower job grade. The final ranking is checked constantly to ensure that it is consistent and accurately reflects the relationship between all the company's jobs, makes sense to the company, and reflects the market accurately.

Considerations for Rank-to-Market Job Evaluation

How Precise Is the Method? Ranking to market is a very direct method of evaluating jobs. It reflects the labor market for high technology jobs, but not the strong performance values of the company's key leader. Because it deals with the whole job, the method does not specifically describe the reasons why one job is ranked higher than another in any terms other than its worth in the labor market.

Job worth is addressed in general rather than specific terms because the external market is the prime determinant of job worth. The ranking of jobs on which survey data are not available is determined on the basis of whether one job is larger or smaller than another. If precision or the ability to use its SPVs is an objective of a company seeking a job evaluation method, ranking to market does not fill the bill.

How Credible Is the Method? One of the strongest arguments made for ranking to market as a form of job evaluation in high technology companies is that it directly reflects the labor market. Although this can be considered the most important element in the determination of the worth of jobs to a company, in companies that want to emphasize their SPVs, this element will not contribute to its credibility for top executives.

Some top executives want to be able to tell managers that their jobs are ranked according to survey information on how similar jobs in other companies are paid. For those companies that are most concerned about how competitively they pay their personnel, the provision of accurate and current management compensation data may be one of the most important features of a job evaluation method. The leaders of these companies may view such a feature as the best way to answer managers' concerns about their pay.

How Easily Can New Jobs Be Integrated? If ranking that compares all management jobs can be done, integrating new management jobs into the system in the future should be fairly easy to do. However, if the new jobs are part of a new technology, obtaining sufficient market information on their worth may be difficult. The rank-to-market system is not exact in its measurement and deals loosely with job content. Because of this, and because the market-ranking system is simple and direct, placing new or changing jobs into an existing job ranking system is a fairly simple task.

However, many companies are concerned about using a more scientific approach to job evaluation—one that makes finer distinctions between jobs and measures SPVs—and a method that merely ranks jobs to other jobs may not satisfy their need for more exacting job comparisons.

Can the Method Adapt to Organizational Changes? Because ranking to market involves whole job ranking, if elements of one job become a part of a second job due to changes in the structure of the company, determining how much the second job increased in worth compared to the first will be difficult. On the other hand, if exacting comparisons are not viewed as important, the relationship of the jobs can be changed fairly easily.

Many executives of companies that use, or have used, market ranking believe that the system cannot reflect the increasing complexities of the jobs in a growing organization. Also, they are concerned about how accurately the system, once instituted, can compare jobs with changing contents. They want to ensure that jobs of equal value are being compared accurately and thoroughly.

Increasing organizational complexity and company growth are the common reasons that executives seek something other than ranking to market for the evaluation of their companies' management jobs. However, the system remains a working and viable alternative as long as accurate market information is available and jobs can be compared on a whole-job basis.

How Difficult Is the Method to Administer? When an organization is small, ranking to market is the ideal system from an administrative standpoint because jobs can be ranked against each other easily, record keeping is simple, and the system is easy to manage. Because ranking-to-market is fairly uncomplicated, it often is the first approach to job evaluation a company selects. However, as a company grows, and the span and scope of its management jobs increase, the rank-to-market system becomes more difficult to administer. This can raise questions with regard to its long-term credibility.

How Does the System Account for Internal and External Worth? Although ranking one whole management job compared to others is a rough methodology for determining the relative internal worth of the job, it does not provide information that describes why the job is of more or less value than other management jobs.

Technical management jobs usually are viewed as complex because of their many components. Rank-to-market does not permit fine comparisons to be made and, therefore, is not able to reflect the SPVs of technical management jobs. For this reason, the system does not account for the internal worth of jobs in high technology companies.

The system is highly responsive to the external market because it uses the market as its evaluation tool. Jobs are likely to be ranked the same way they are in companies included in surveys of management jobs, and two market ranking companies that exchange information on management pay are likely to have management jobs with very similar relationships. However, the external market does not reflect the cultures or performance values of individual companies. Unless a company's sole purpose is to identify the external market place worth of its jobs, market ranking can leave something to be desired.

How Easy Is the Method to Communicate? In its simplest form, market ranking is easy to communicate. Because the market is the only yardstick that is used to judge job worth, key leaders can tell managers that the external market determines the worth of their jobs. If top management wants to link the company's strong performance values to its evaluation system, however, effective communication of the system becomes more difficult. Also, when management jobs become more complex, or when leaders want salaries to represent something other than the external labor market (in other words, an internal value), the communication of ranking to market to managers becomes less simple.

Can Market Ranking Be Used for Other Purposes? Ranking to market ranks management jobs to the market and to each other; it does not identify any reason why one job is more or less valuable than another except the reason that the jobs are so ranked in the market. Thus, this system does not have any other application in human resource management.

The Essential Features

The market ranking plan depends on accurate survey information. Regression analysis provides companies with a more sophisticated, statistical method of determining what a job is worth. The use of regression analysis is increasing; as a result, it is essential that companies have fresh and accurate survey data on comparable jobs within an industry. Given the rapidly changing nature of the high technology market, however, maintaining up-to-date survey data may be impossible.

Although accurate market data provide an external justification for job ranking, a company must document the internal reasons for the ranking of its jobs. A record of the system preserves its credibility and communicates the reasons for the ranking to employees. Often, the preparation of such a record leads the company to the identification of compensable factors—that is, what it is about one job that makes it more or less valuable to the company than another. Compensable factors reflect a rationale for the job ranking and may identify critical SPVs. It is possible that the process of documenting the rank-to-market system may lead the company to develop other forms of job evaluation, such as those reviewed in the next sections.

Point-Factor Job Evaluation

The point-factor method is a quantitative job evaluation plan. With this plan, several compensable factors the company believes should determine the value of its management jobs are identified. The factors can include the company's SPVs and reflect the culture of the organization. Each job is then assigned a numerical score that represents the sum total of all the job's compensable factors, and a total point score is calculated for all management jobs. The total point scores are assigned to salary ranges that convert the scores into market values, thereby placing the jobs in competitive salary levels.

In a point-factor plan, several compensable factors (or job characteristics) that are present in all management jobs in the company are selected. Each factor is described clearly, and factor levels also are defined. Each factor level receives a specific number of points. A management job is evaluated on each factor, according to the level of the factor that best describes the job. Once a management job has been evaluated on all compensable factors, its total point score is calculated. When all jobs are evaluated, they can be ranked from high to low, based on their total point scores.

To ensure that the point-factor plan will predict the market as accurately as possible, top management selects factors that reflect the market, such as financial job scope, impact on the profits of the company, technical decision-making responsibility, and so forth, on the basis of their consistency with the performance values and culture of the organization.

Two criteria are used to determine the number of points that are assigned to factor levels. One is how well the compensable factor determines salary and the other is how responsive the resultant salary is to the external labor market. The criteria are based on survey data obtained on a sample of management benchmark jobs. Using standard regression analysis, the best combination of factor weights and the best number of points for each factor are found. The total points a job receives from the job evaluation process are converted to actual dollar amounts. Keeping salary levels fairly close to market salary information is necessary if the company is to attract qualified new managers. Because of this, a job's internal worth should reflect its external value as determined by what salary grade is considered competitive in the market place.

Steps in a Point-Factor Plan

As do all job evaluation plans, the point-factor plan needs accurate job information, which can be obtained by the administering of position questionnaires or other methods. Job analysis usually is performed on the basis of the compensable factors determined by top management.

Compensable factors may measure a job on its financial performance; its accountability for technical excellence; the contacts inside and outside the company that are important to the performance of the job; its planning, organizing, and coordinating functions; and the business problem solving it requires. In most cases, no more than five or six compensable factors are needed to measure all management jobs in a company. Overlap of compensable factors should be eliminated as much as possible.

Each compensable factor is defined carefully. It is important to describe the factor in terminology commonly used in the company to minimize confusion. Introducing new terminology will increase communications difficulties.

After the factors have been defined, levels are determined for each factor. Care must be taken to make sure there is a smooth transition between each level of a compensable factor. The terminology used should define each level in a way that clearly differentiates it from the levels above and below it. In most cases, six to nine factor levels are identified.

One way to determine the worth of factor levels is to assign each level a letter value. For example, the first level is assigned an *A,* the second a *B,* and so forth. To differentiate within a level, a plus or minus sign may be used. When the *A* is shown as an A − or an A +, this indicates that the job falls between two factor levels.

Survey or benchmark jobs are evaluated first. When this step in the evaluation is complete, all bench mark jobs will have been assigned letter values for each factor. For example, one job may have been assigned a C + on a factor that reflects the job's scope, a D − on a factor that reflects the contacts needed to perform the job, and so forth.

At this point, regression analysis is used to convert the letter value to point values. Each job's point values are then added together for a total point score, which places the job in a grade that is consistent with the market. The final step of the plan is to evaluate all remaining management jobs and establish a salary structure.

Many point-factor plans preweight the compensable factors and assign each factor level a point value before any jobs are evaluated. For example, top management may decide that the compensable factor designed to reflect the contacts necessary to perform a management job is worth 25 percent of the total point score, while the factor that reflects the technical knowledge needed by the incumbent is worth 30 percent of the total point score. This approach may accurately reflect internal job worth, but if the external world values the compensable factors differently, the final results of the evaluation will not correspond with the market. This difference is not improper if the company values a particular factor much more or much less than the market does. A company with an SPVC, for instance, may decide that a specific SPV is so important as a compensable factor that it chooses to ignore the market value of the factor. However, even companies with strong performance value cultures and well-communicated performance values may want the results of their job evaluation programs to match both internal and external realities.

Considerations for Point-Factor Plans

A point-factor plan measures the worth of a job through the use of a set of compensable factors that should reflect the strong performance values of the company. While ranking to market compares each whole job with each other whole job, point-factor plans identify several important elements of job worth and compare each job on the basis of these elements.

How Precise Is the Approach? Some key leaders believe that one advantage of the point-factor method is its ability to reduce the evaluation of each job to its compensable elements. They believe that if jobs are compared according to a series of common elements, according to the extent to which those elements vary in importance from job to job, the comparison will be more exact. As was suggested earlier, in many ways, when the company begins to prepare a log that explains the ranking of whole jobs in a rank-to-market plan, it is in the first stage of defining compensable factors.

Because point-factor plans define the reasons one job is more important than another, they can reflect a company's SPVs. In addition, if the factor weighting reflects market values, the job evaluation will place jobs in competitive salary ranges.

Is the System Credible? To the extent that the company is successful in selecting compensable factors that reflect corporate performance values and differentiate between the worth of management jobs, the system will be credible. If the company designs the system so that the results of the internal evaluation places jobs in ranges that represent the realities of the high technology market, the credibility of the point-factor plan is assured. If a plan does not use compensable factors that specifically reflect the characteristics of the company—for example, if the factors a high technology company uses are the same as those used by steel mills—the plan will not have credible results.

Because point-factor plans reflect the worth of jobs in quantitative terms and engineers and scientists have a strong bias toward the use of mathematical solutions to problems, well-designed point-factor plans often are accepted easily by high technology managers. The results of a method that uses yardsticks that are designed to reflect the performance values and culture of the individual company numerically can be explained in terms managers will believe readily. In addition, because the method makes finer job comparisons than do systems that attempt to deal with whole jobs, managers will accept that the resultant differentiations between jobs are accurate.

Integration of New Jobs. If a job evaluation plan is designed to cover a complete range of possible management functions, it will be easy to integrate new and changing jobs into the system. However, if the terminology of the factors cannot accurately differentiate between the worth of existing and the worth of new jobs, the integration of new jobs into the system will be very difficult. It is not possible to change existing compensable factors or to add new factors without reevaluating all managment jobs currently in the system. Thus, the plan must be designed initially to evaluate all possible jobs.

To the extent that the existing factors, factor levels, and their relationships to the market place are designed with the expectation that the company may add jobs, the system will be very flexible. However, key leaders say that lack of flexibility is the main reason for the failure of a point-factor system. A plan will not reflect the changing nature of a company if it does not permit the custom selection and definition of factors to meet the evolving needs of the company or if it uses inflexible terminology that is foreign to any aspect of the industry.

Point-Factor Plans and Organizational Changes. A number of point-factor plans use the words *organization, group, division,* and *unit* to denote on what level within the company a compensable factor has the most impact. These terms mean different things to different companies. In the event of organizational changes, the words' meanings may change within the company. When the plan's terminology is inflexible, the method will not be able to respond to the changes in organizational structure that are common in growing high technology companies. Avoiding any terminology that would become obsolete if a company changes is essential if the point-factor plan is to be responsive to growth and change.

When a point-factor plan is well designed, it can help an organization have smooth transitions in a period of change by identifying how its jobs have altered in content as a result of reassignment of duties. For instance, because a job's assigned duties and responsibilities are measured by compensable factors, when duties change, the job's value is reassessed easily. The plan aids in the realignment of jobs and in the communication of changes in job worth throughout the company.

How Difficult Is a Point-Factor Plan to Administer? The use of small computers or large information systems has eliminated much of the manual work that, historically, has been associated with administrating and updating job evaluation plans. When a computer is used, the job evaluation system can be included as a part of the company's management information system, thereby simplifying its administration.

With manual administration, however, the point-factor plan is cumbersome. A point-factor plan is more difficult to administer manually than is a rank-to-market plan.

Accounting for Internal and External Worth. If the point-factor plan is designed so that the total point scores for each job will result in the job's being placed in a salary range that is consistent with what the external world pays comparable jobs, the system is an excellent reconciliation of a job's internal worth with its external worth. Plans developed this way can be adjusted to reflect the labor market without necessitating the reevaluation of all jobs. The adjustment is done by repointing the plan—assigning new point values to factor weights and levels—which results in the placement of jobs in new salary ranges that reflect the changed market values.

How Easy Is the Plan to Communicate? Point-factor plans introduce a concept that may be foreign to managers unless their company has SPVs. By their nature, these plans use the same compensable factors to evaluate all jobs. If these factors are commonly viewed as the elements that are most important in determining what a job is worth (as the key leader's strong performance values are viewed in a company with an SPVC), the plan will be easy to communicate. Satisfied users say that being able to tell managers that all jobs are evaluated according to the same elements of job worth is an advantage from the standpoint of communications.

Problems arise, however, when managers believe that some important elements that determine the worth of management jobs have been omitted from the plan. The plan cannot be changed readily once it has been installed, and if the original factors do not reflect what managers believe are important aspects of their jobs, the communications effort will be thwarted.

Effective communications describe the logic of point-factor plans. They stress that the determination of job worth is a well-organized process and they show how the plan can be used effectively to differentiate between jobs and create a competitive pay structure. The fact that the quantitative nature of point-factor plans is popular with engineering and scientific managers also helps the communications effort.

Can a Point-Factor Plan Be Used for Other Purposes? Point-factor plans, like market ranking plans, usually are used only for job evaluation. The compensable factors may have some value in the area of performance appraisal, although they usually are not specific enough to serve as the basis for relevant job standards and requirements. Those plans that are designed to measure the impact of management jobs on the achievement of SPVs, with the SPVs used as compensable factors, however, may have many applications in the area of human resource management.

The Essential Features

Some key leaders object to the fact that many job evaluation plans have no use other than the evaluation of jobs. They believe that the time and effort such programs require should yield something more than merely a program to evaluate jobs. This is why a job evaluation plan should be linked to the SPVC of the company. Compensable factors that reflect SPVs communicate those values during the job evaluation process.

The availability of job information and market data is important to a point-factor plan, just as it is important to any method of job evaluation. However, the point-factor plan can deal more easily with management jobs on which specific survey information is not available, and it is not essential that survey data verify the validity of the evaluation. Because the jobs are broken down into their compensable elements, a single yardstick is used to compare all jobs. This requires, of course, that the factors be defined clearly and accurately. The definition of the factors and their levels must be consistent with the way the company talks about the worth of its management jobs. Because performance values are communicated through the factor definitions, it makes no sense to introduce a foreign terminology in the evaluation of jobs. Compensable factors that have proven useful elsewhere, especially those that are supposed to be universal to any industry, will not reflect a company's specific strong performance values. Accurate factor selection and definition, then, is essential to effective point-factor evaluation.

Key leaders must be responsible for the appropriateness of the compensable factors and factor-level definitions. They must make them measure their firm's strong performance values. The best way to ensure their appropriateness is to test the compensable factors on a sample of management jobs. This testing usually is accomplished when the benchmark jobs are evaluated. Once tested and applied, the factors should be reviewed periodically to make sure that they continue to reflect the values of the company. The point-factor plan's strength rests in its use of a stable and constant yardstick (the factors) to measure jobs. This yardstick needs careful attention and continued grooming in order for the plan to work effectively.

Knowledge and Abilities Job Evaluation

High technology tinkerers may try to utilize the performance values, skills, knowledge, and abilities needed to perform each management job in designing a job-evaluation plan. Ralph Ellis may have pioneered this idea.[1] Ellis seemed to be an early tinkerer, not in the high technology industry since it did not exist at that time, but in general management. He suggested that the compensable factors used to evaluate jobs could be the abilities and knowledge each job required. Although he only addressed the problem of evaluating nonmanagement jobs, the application of the concept may be broadened to deal with a few of the shortcomings identified in the systems of job evaluation discussed so far.

The use of knowledge and abilities required by the jobs as compensable factors is a qualitative rather than a quantitative approach to job evaluation. The approach does not rely solely on data from an external market, nor on points or statistical analysis. The applicability of the yardstick of knowledge and abilities depends on the content of the jobs to be evaluated; that is, it depends on how much knowledge and ability is needed to perform the management jobs. Unlike in the point-factor plan, in this approach the value of the knowledge and abilities is determined separately from the value of individual jobs. The value of the knowledge and abilities is determined and subsequently assigned to jobs. The sum of the value of knowledge and abilities results in the value of the job.

Steps to Knowledge and Abilities Job Evaluation

As is the case with rank-to-market and point-factor job evaluation plans, accurate survey data and job information are needed in the job evaluation method that uses knowledge and abilities as its form of measurement. Job information may be obtained from formal job descriptions or completed job questionnaires. The survey of key and benchmark jobs must be conducted so that job content, rather than titles, is compared.

The first step is to identify and define the knowledge and abilities that are necessary for the performance of the jobs. For example, one job may require knowledge of high technology management practices, another may require the ability to exercise independent scientific judgment, and a third may require knowledge of accounting theory and practice. The knowledge and abilities can (and should) be related to the company's SPVs.

Once identified, the knowledge and abilities should be described, in writing, in a way that makes them clearly understandable in the context of the company. As might be expected, a number of the types of knowledge and the abilities identified and defined will be applicable to all management jobs in a company, while others will be applicable only to some of the jobs. Knowledge and abilities that are both general and specific should be used to determine the value of the jobs. Once the types of knowledge and the abilities are identified and defined, they are listed randomly to separate them from the management jobs that require them. This attempts to eliminate any bias that may occur when a job with a known incumbent is being evaluated. At the end of this step, a complete list of what is needed to perform management jobs in a specific company should exist.

Next, the knowledge and abilities are evaluated by the senior managers who have a thorough understanding of the management process within the company. The system, in its pure form, does not utilize points in assigning value to compensable elements; rather, each type of knowledge and each ability is rated on the basis of its level of difficulty. The committee of senior managers rates the abilities and types of knowledge. Usually only three difficulty levels are used, because it is easier to determine whether something belongs in one of a few difficulty categories than it is to determine whether it belongs in one of many categories. The product of this step is a list of well-described types of knowledge and abilities, each rated according to its level of difficulty.

At this point, the types of knowledge and abilities are returned to the jobs from which they were obtained. One job may have six very difficult types of knowledge or abilities, three of moderate difficulty, and one that is less difficult. Another job may have five very difficult, three moderately difficult, and two fairly easy abilities or types of knowledge. A job hierarchy is created, with the jobs that require the most difficult types of knowledge and abilities at the top and those that require the least difficult at the bottom.

The last step of the plan is to build a salary structure. The benchmark jobs and regression analysis may be used to convert the number of types of knowledge and abilities necessary to perform a job into a market value. For example, the job with twelve very difficult types of knowledge and abilities might be in grade twenty-five, the jobs with ten or eleven very difficult types of knowledge and abilities might be in grade twenty-four, and so forth.

This system uses the specific elements needed to perform management jobs to evaluate the worth of all jobs (and possibly their impact on the achievement of SPVs). Unlike with the point-factor plan, however, when new types of knowledges and abilities develop, or existing ones change, they can be added to the system without changing the results of the evaluation. Also, the system may be used to evaluate or reevaluate only a portion of the company if the new types of knowledge and abilities apply only to part of the organization. Because the knowledge and abilities need not be common to all management jobs, each job can be evaluated on the basis of the specific skills necessary to perform that job. It is not necessary to evaluate all jobs on the same set of compensable factors, and, therefore, the application of the method does not strain the semantics of the elements by applying them too broadly.

Considerations for the Use of Knowledge and Abilities

The system that uses knowledge and abilities differs from the other job evaluation plans because it deals with the content of each management job and does not require that a single yardstick be developed to measure all jobs. Also, it may be able to deal with the peculiarities of management jobs (as opposed to other jobs in the company) and present the compensable elements in terms of acutal skills.

How Precise Is the Method? Because the system does not use either whole-job ranking or a set of compensable factors for all jobs, it is as precise as the definition of the requirements of the specific management jobs to be evaluated. This approach seems to be consistent with what the tinkerers in companies with strong performance-value cultures are trying to do.

How Credible Is the Method? Because the system uses types of knowledge and abilities that managers recognize as necessary for the effective performance of their jobs, managers are likely to view the system as a relevant way of evaluating their jobs. This approach does not introduce any elements that are not already in the company; all it does is identify and define the existing elements in terms of what they contribute to the performance of jobs. As long as the terminology used to define the required knowledge and abilities is acceptable, the method will be credible. In addition, because the elements can be redefined as management jobs change, the method offers long-term credibility.

Integration of New Jobs. Because new types of knowledge and new abilities can be added, the system is receptive to new and changing jobs. The system need not be changed in the event a new technology is introduced into the management process, and new jobs, along with their attendant compensable elements, can be added to the structure. The program will not become obsolete when jobs change.

Adapting to Organizational Changes. Because the system does not depend on a fixed set of compensable elements, organizational and structural changes that cause the reassignment of knowledge and abilities and the development of new knowledge and abilities will not disrupt the basic system. This approach is designed around the content of specific jobs and it can be expanded to new knowledge and abilities, whether they are added requirements of existing jobs or they are the requirements of new jobs.

Ease of Administration. The system, like the point-factor plan, is fairly complex to administer manually. The use of computers makes the system less cumbersome to apply and provides clerical support. The identification and definition of the types of knowledge and abilities is a time-consuming process that must be done by senior management, not by a computer. However, in the companies with strong performance value cultures, this step of the method allows key leaders to phrase the elements in a way that communicates the performance values to the managers.

Accounting for External and Internal Worth. This method deals directly with the content of each management job and so addresses the worth of the jobs to the company. It directly associates what is necessary for the performance of the management job with the evaluation of the job. A type of knowledge or an ability has the same value no matter which job requires it. No important job element will be overlooked. Thus, the system thoroughly and validly accounts for internal worth.

The system provides for the evaluation of benchmark jobs on which survey data are available. Subsequently, jobs are placed in salary ranges that reflect external market values. However, the system is less directly associated with the market than is the rank-to-market method, which uses the market to determine job value, or the point-factor plans, which may use the market to determine factor weights.

Communicating Knowledge and Abilities. Because a system of this type deals directly with the content of management jobs (and, hopefully, the SPVs of the company), if it is designed to accurately identify the elements needed to perform the jobs, it should be hightly credible and easy to communicate. The specific responsibilities, of which managers are already aware, are used to evaluate the jobs, so, unless the terminology used to describe the elements is unfamiliar to them, managers should have no trouble understanding the system.

Other Purposes. Job evaluation is only one of the possible applications for the system. The elements of each job also may be used to develop a job profile for performance appraisal. If a knowledge of engineering theory and practice is identified as a compensable element, it also can be used in performance appraisal because it appears only in jobs that require this knowledge. This will link the performance appraisal process and the job evaluation process and may help to solve some of the problems performance appraisal systems have faced for years. Few existing performance systems are able to associate the reasons for compensation with the criteria used to evaluate the performance of the incumbents. The use of knowledge and abilities as compensable factors allows this association to be made.

In companies where leaders are interested in establishing career paths for the continuing development of employees, the system may provide the method they need. Establishing and communicating the route to more responsible jobs in terms of the knowledge and abilities the jobs require enables the individuals who are seeking to follow specific career paths to identify what they must learn to grow in their professional areas and to progress within the organization.

The Essential Features

The success of the knowledge and abilities system depends on the accurate identification of the types of knowledge and the abilities required by jobs in the high technology company. The key leader and other top managers who understand the performance values and the role of management in their specific company must invest a great deal of time in identifying and defining the elements. Once this has been accomplished, however, the method has applications beyond job evaluation.

The approach can associate the job evaluation program with other human resource management systems. In particular, it can directly relate the criteria for job evaluation with the criteria for employee performance appraisal.

Summary

Job evaluation plans help companies to establish what their management jobs are worth. It is important that high technology companies use an approach that can be modified to reflect the culture of the individual company as well as the dynamic nature of the industry. This may require them to use both a program based on compensable elements that effectively communicate their corporate values and a program that relies on market data. Companies no longer need to accept a single approach; complex problems may require complex solutions. Companies now may select one job evaluation method and modify it to fit the way they do things or they may select two or more approaches and create hybrids tailored to their needs.

Note

1. Ralph W. Ellis, *The Basic Abilities System of Job Evaluation.* (Madison: Bureau of Business Research and Service, University of Wisconsin, 1951).

5 Management Short-Term Incentives

Nearly all for-profit corporations have some form of incentive compensation for management personnel. The companies with SPVCs use these plans to communicate and reinforce their strong performance values. To do this, a company must integrate its performance priorities with the design of the plan it uses to administer financial rewards. The most effective incentive plan communicates both the qualitative and quantitative yardsticks the company uses to measure its performance. All successful compensation plans, including incentive plans, reflect the cultures of their corporate users and reinforce those companies' strong performance values.

Management Incentive Practices

Short-term incentive plans are very popular in high technology companies. Most of these companies view incentives as an essential feature of management compensation. Short-term incentives are awarded in recognition of performance that can be measured within a short period of time, and they are popular because they are flexible. Many companies tie their plans as closely as possible to the attainment of specific organizational and individual goals and vary incentive awards according to how well their managers attain such goals.

A number of incentive programs are used to supplement base salaries. In other words, the company views the total cash compensation a manager receives as the sum of base salary and incentive award(s). This is a competitive practice, which indicates that the awarding of short-term incentives is common.

Originally, many incentive plans were discretionary. Presently, there seems to be a trend toward the formalization of short-term plans, and incentives often are awarded on the basis of performance defined or measured by preset financial targets. Performance criteria are established to make the granting of an incentive contingent upon corporate financial performance over which the management group is supposed to have some direct control.

The management incentive plans in companies with SPVCs are designed to reward performance that is consistent with both qualitative and quantitative criteria. To communicate a company's SPVs and support its SPVC, a program must be developed to reflect the nature of that specific company—it should not be a copy of plans used by other companies, which may have different cultures. In many instances, special award programs that recognize significant contributions after the fact publicize the reasons for the award in order to communicate to other managers that good performance is worthwhile financially.

The mix of base salary and annual incentive awards varies from company to company. Some companies believe that cash compensation should come principally from base salary and view the incentive award as an extra source of compensation. Other companies believe that as much as half of a manager's total cash compensation should come from an annual incentive plan. These companies' compensation plans generally provide that a meaningful amount of managers' cash compensation is at risk and dependent on some measure of organizational, group, or individual performance.

Incentive Plan Participation

It is the responsibility of the key leader to determine employees' eligibility for incentive plan participation. Top management should establish guidelines for plan participation. The jobs and people that will be eligible for incentive plan participation must be identified. When an organization is small, managers may be included on a discretionary basis. However, as the firm grows and becomes more complex, the discretionary approach becomes more cumbersome and inequities often emerge. The need for formal guidelines that define eligibility requirements increases as a company grows. Once a job or a manager has been included in an incentive plan, however, senior management may be hesitant to disqualify that job or manager in the future. It is very difficult to take incentive participation away from managers or jobs once they have become eligible. As a result, participation may expand to the point where management feels that the plan is too extensive.

In many instances, companies try to limit participation to jobs that might have an impact on the performance of the organization as a whole. In other instances, the impact of a job on the performance of some smaller organizational unit within the company is a criterion for eligibility. Key leaders generally believe that participation in incentive plans is good as long as acceptable guidelines are used to determine the awarding of incentives. The high technology companies that have SPVCs design their annual incentive plans to include as many managers that might have an impact on the attainment of their strong performance values as possible. The key leaders of these companies believe that incentives are the most powerful and flexible communications tool available for the reinforcement of strong performance values.

Some of the most frequently used guidelines for incentive plan eligibility include management job grade, reporting level, pay level, job title, and, in a few cases, length of service with the company. The criteria that key managers believe work the best are those that base elibility on reporting level. Although most executives recognize that reporting level and impact on corporate performance may not be directly related, they view reporting level as a good starting point for determining the extent to which a management job can have impact on the short-term success of the company. Executives believe that other eligibility criteria can cause confusion and inequities. For instance, job title is a more subjective criterion for incentive eligibility than is reporting level. Companies that use management pay grade as the guideline for incentive eligibility indicate that this often places excessive upward pressure on the management base pay structure.

A number of companies use a combination of reporting level and nomination by an executive committee to determine incentive eligibility. With this approach, an individual may not participate automatically in the incentive plan each year just because his or her management job is at a specific level. This combination of criteria makes plan participation less automatic and awards those management jobs that may not be positioned at the required reporting level, but that may have significant impact on the company's financial performance and the attainment of SPVs.

Incentives and Taxes

Most short-term incentive awards for managers are paid in cash or stock at the end of the performance period. The award incurs a tax obligation to the recipient. In some instances the recipient may voluntarily defer some or all of the incentive award. The deferral is offered to provide the recipient with the opportunity to postpone the tax obligations incurred as a result of the award to some future year when the manager's taxable income may be reduced, such as after retirement. Those who defer are hoping that the tax obligation will occur during a year when they will be in a lower tax bracket. The problem with this hope is that managers can never be certain that taxes will not subsequently increase. Managers that elect to defer their incentive awards may be moving their tax obligation to a year in which they will be taxed at an even higher rate.

In the companies that provide for the voluntary deferral of short-term incentive awards, in order to avoid the possible tax consequences of the doctrine of constructive receipt, managers must elect to defer their award as much as twelve to fourteen months before it is announced. The objective of short-term incentive plans is to reward current performance; concern about tax consequences may detract from the positive impact and the timeliness of the award. Because of this, companies should think twice before they bring up the award's tax implications. The incentive to continue to perform well may be depleted by the manager's desire to minimize the tax consequences of an incentive award.

Among the managers who have the option to defer, few seem to take advantage of it. Concern regarding the interpretation of the doctrine of constructive receipt, which provides that if the manager has actually received the award, he or she cannot refuse it and thereby delay its tax obligations, may, therefore, be unnecessary.

Incentive Performance Criteria

Most short-term incentive plans are based at least partially on some measure of corporate, group, or divisional financial performance. In many instances, the company's current performance and its performance in prior years, or its current performance and the current performance of its industry group, are compared on the basis of financial criteria. Executives understand, however, that financial information does not always reflect what is going on in a company or industry. When measuring performance, the more sophisticated top managers want to use measures that are not subject to differences in accounting methodology or are not affected by inflation. Key leaders have expressed a need for measures that reflect the real growth or worth of their companies. The need for such criteria is not limited to the area of short-term incentives; long-term incentives also need better measures.

Some of the popular financial criteria used today include:

1. Earnings per share. This measure is favored widely because it is reported on companies' financial statements. The figure is the company's net income divided by the average number of shares of common stock outstanding.
2. Return on equity. This measure is the company's net income divided by the average of shareholders' equity (common and preferred stock, plus retained earnings).
3. Return on capital. This measure is computed by dividing the company's net income by its average capital (shareholders' equity plus outstanding loans).
4. Return on assets. This measure is calculated by dividing the net income of the company by its net sales.

Specific complaints about these criteria abound. The major concern, however, is that a financial measure does not give a complete portrayal of a company's performance.

Many important contributions are not reflected financially for years. In addition, managers may have no control over the results shown by financial criteria. Measuring manager performance on the basis of such criteria, then, results in inaccurate evaluations. Using a combination of qualitative and quantitative measures of company and individual performance should account for any shortcomings of either set of criteria when used alone.

Currently, research is being conducted to identify measures of corporate financial performance that will reflect the worth of a company accurately. Executive compensation planners are seeking factors that better reflect the future profitability of companies. Their approach emphasizes the development of long-range corporate plans. In coming years, it is likely that the financial interests of the manager will be tied more closely to the interests of the company's shareholders. Boards of directors are becoming more and more concerned about the design of management compensation programs. They want their plans to be reasonable and consistent with the real performance of their companies. They want the efforts of their managers to benefit both the managers themselves and the shareholders. One way to link the interests of shareholders and managers financially is to award stock or stock options to those managers who make a significant contribution to the company.

Shareholders have a right to a reasonable return on investment, because the only way shareholders can gain from their investment in a company is through the appreciation of the value of the stock or by receiving the dividends paid by the company. In most high technology companies, during the early years shareholders' gains comes more from stock appreciation, because much of the money that could be paid as dividends is retained by the company and invested in further growth. Once the company is established, however, its key leaders and board members will want the shareholders to have first claim on any profits the company makes. This means that a specific level of profits must be generated by the company before the incentive plan can begin to pay out awards.

If the relationship between the management team and the shareholders is to be a healthy one, managers should have a "him first and then me" attitude toward sharing in the financial success of the company. The shareholders usually will compare their return on investment in the company with the returns on their other investments to judge how well the company is doing. The only way to ensure that shareholders will receive competitive returns on their investment and that managers will be rewarded for their contributions is to have a successful company. This must be communicated to managers and all employees through the incentive plan and other communications channels. In this way the concept of "cooperative winning" is communicated not only within the company but also to the investment community. Where everybody has a chance to win, financial success seems worthwhile.

Incentive Award Size

Executives should keep at least two principles in mind when determining the parameters of financial awards. The most important is that the award granted should be consistent with the recipient's contribution to the company. A significant contribution is worth a significant financial reward. Top management must show that they back the concept of the incentive plan. The second principle is related to the first: the reward must be worth going after. A reward must appear significant to the manager who is working to receive it. A lot of time and money is spent on the design of a financial reward system. If that system does not provide the managers with the opportunity to earn meaningful rewards, the expenditure is senseless.

Minimum Incentive Awards

Minimum and maximum award amounts usually are established to define the limits for the actual awards managers can receive. Setting a minimum amount is reasonable because an award that amounts to 2 or 3 percent of base salary or less is not worth much effort. Some compensation plan designers believe that no award that amounts to less than 5 percent of base salary should be granted, while others say that awards should be at least 8 to 10 percent of base salary.

The rule probably should be based on a minimum performance level set by the company. This level can be seen as the threshold—the point at which the manager becomes eligible for participation in the incentive plan. Even at the minimal level, some performance "stretch" should exist. In other words, the plan must require that managers expend effort to obtain an incentive. If the performance threshold is selected well, it seems reasonable to conclude that no award of less than 5 percent of base salary would be viewed as meaningful by the manager. The plan that cannot provide an award equal to 5 percent of base salary as soon as threshold performance is exceeded would, therefore, not be worthwhile.

Maximum Incentive Awards

Maximum incentive award amounts can be controversial. In some instances, maximum award limits are established to ensure that payments from the incentive plan will not get out of hand. The plan designers may feel they are not able to set accurate performance targets. If actual performance exeeds the incentive plan objectives, the discrepancy may be because the targets were set too low rather than because manager performance was exceptional. If an incentive award reflects poorly set performance goals, it may be unreasonably large (or small) with respect to the manager's contribution.

The compensation planning process should avoid setting a maximum incentive award. Telling managers that there is a cap on the incentive plan is a very negative communication. There is no cap on the upside of corporate performance, after all, and if managers are to be members of the team that shares in the company's success, or lack of it, the incentive plan should communicate the message that outstanding performance will be recognized by an outstanding reward.

If maximum amounts for incentive awards are established, the amounts must be consistent with the risk the manager has to take in order to attain the award. Companies that need a general rule for a cap should start somewhere in the vicinity of 50 percent of base salary.

No cap should be used as an excuse for not making an award if circumstances beyond the control of the manager caused performance objectives to be missed. Companies seldom grant awards when overall corporate performance has been poor—regardless of how well individual managers or groups performed. If awards are not to be granted because the company did poorly, that is the reason that should be communicated to employees. The existence and amount of the cap should be broadcast when it is set so that no confusion arises when it is exercised.

Special Award Programs

Special incentive award programs are popular with key leaders in the high technology industry. Interest in these plans is particularly high in companies with strong performance-value cultures that perform at the highest levels. Special award programs are designed to reward significant, innovative contributions that were not planned for. These plans recognize contributions beyond those provided for in other incentive plans. Special award programs also permit companies to recognize the contributions of managers who may not be eligible to participate in the formal incentive plan. Such programs provide companies with maximum flexibility in their recognition of significant contributions.

Special award plans usually are designed to grant a financial award immediately following the employee's significant performance. The timing of the reward reinforces the value of the performance. Because the program grants special awards in a highly visible way, it communicates the financial worth of good performance to all employees, not just the recipient.

In most cases, special awards are fairly large. In the high technology companies surveyed in the research for the book, awards ranged from 10 to 20 percent of base salary.

Special award plans should supplement those formal management-incentive plans that are not flexible enough to recognize all forms of re-wardable performance or cannot make rewards in a timely fashion. Special awards also may be used to show managers that contributions outside the parameters of the company's standard performance criteria are financially worthwhile.

Measuring Management Contribution

It would be ideal if credible incentive plans that directly reward the contri-butions of individual managers could be designed. Because the management process in high technology companies often requires the close integration of various professional staff and operating units, it usually is not possible for these companies to consistently separate the performance of one manager from that of another. The companies benefit the most if managers are rewarded on the basis of their cooperation and teamwork rather than on their individual performance. Rewards that financially recognize individ-uals' contributions to the team effort emphasize cooperation and the exchanging of ideas.

Some companies are committed to rewarding individual performance, while others, usually the organizations with strong performance-value cul-tures, emphasize the performance of groups. Groups to be so evaluated may be defined organizational units in a single discipline or cross-functional or cross-discipline units. The companies that reward teamwork and value the individual who can work well with others tend to be those companies that perform the most successfully in the high technology industry.

In most companies, a combination of individual and group perfor-mance is necessary for sustained financial success. Individual creativity helps the company stay ahead in a dynamic technology, but only if it is operationalized. It often takes more than one individual to operationalize or take full advantage of a great idea. Performance criteria, then, must reward both individual and organizational performance and discourage internal activity that is disruptive to the organization. Using both qualita-tive and quantitative yardsticks will help to measure both group and indi-vidual performance. The criteria must reinforce top management's perfor-mance values, and if those values stress teamwork, the performance criteria must be credible measures of group cooperation.

Management-Incentive Objectives

Many important strong performance values are expressed in descriptive terms that cannot be converted to numerical performance measures. These qualitative milestones are very important to the attainment of financial performance values, especially in complex high technology companies. More often than not, executives feel that contributions to the achievement of engineering and scientific performance values should be defined and measured qualitatively rather than quantitatively. Some portion of a short-term incentive plan must reward both specific and general performance that either attains short-term goals or represents a milestone toward the attainment of longer-term goals. The final objective may be measured in either financial or nonfinancial terms.

The use of both qualitative and quantitative performance goals will help the reward system to reinforce and communicate strong performance values. The connection between the performance values and the rewards should be accomplished by means of specifically defined strategic and tactical administrative systems.

Executives in high technology companies define performance as the accomplishment of significant tasks that lead to the attainment of profits and other corporate objectives. The organization's key leader must tell the managers/performers what the tasks are and how they should perform them so that the worth of the company to the shareholders will be increased (which, in turn, will result in financial gain to its key contributors). This requires top management to define performance values clearly, to show the managers how to perform in a way that is consistent with the key leader's expectations. In short, it requires management by SPVs.

The inclusion of both financial and written (qualitative) objectives in the performance charter tells potential contributors both the desired end result and the routes that should be pursued to achieve that result. The qualitative objectives often explain the financial ones. For example, if a coach tells an athlete the objective is to run a mile in less than four minutes, this does not help the runner accomplish the objective. If, however, the coach instructs the runner on how to condition his or her body, how to run a smart race, what to do when a strong competitor leans forward at the finish line, and so forth, this useful information tells the athlete what to do to attain the objective. Numerical yardsticks show how well the performers do, but they are of little use in sustaining and improving successful performance. The financial results are the end product of specific milestones that, if they were successful, most likely were described qualitatively, in words rather than in numbers.

Steps to Incentive Plan Design

So far, the need for a job evaluation process and ideas about short-term incentive compensation plans have been discussed. However, an approach that might lead to the successful development of these plans has yet to be suggested. Plan design is a function of matching a successful problem-solving process to the culture of the organization. Once key leaders are accustomed to a workable approach to designing an administrative program, the approach can be used to develop job evaluation, compensation, incentive, and benefit programs.

Short-term incentive plans provide executives with a good, and perhaps the best, opportunity to associate the strong performance values of the company with its financial reward system. The company's SPVs are the rudder for management financial rewards. Companies with strong performance values can communicate and reinforce them through their management compensation plans. Organizations with weak or mixed performance values need to clarify their values before they can design effective management compensation plans. Without strong performance values, companies may manage by a knee-jerk approach to problem solving, with executives moving from crisis to crisis and responding only to the issue perceived as most crucial. Such companies do not have—or are not utilizing—an organized method of gathering information, evaluating alternative solutions, and reaching a solution that is sound from both a short- and a long-term perspective.

For example, in the early 1980s a popular knee-jerk response to recession was to reduce professional staff and change incentive plans in an attempt to reduce costs and increase short-term profits. Instead of stabilizing employment and managing themselves in order to gain technologically, many firms fell further behind because of their preoccupation with short-term financial results. The best performers stuck to their plans, dealt with contingencies in a manner that did not contradict their SPVs, and were rewarded for their tenacity in the long run.

This example should provide companies with an important lesson concerning incentives and company performance values. Before a key leader decides how to reinforce performance, he or she must define the performance priorities of the company. First, the most important performance values must be identified and, second, the midrange or supporting performance values that will lead to the accomplishment of SPVs must be developed. Enough flexibility must be built into the plan to permit changes of course over time as the impact of external forces, such as the economy, changes. All plans must have contingencies that also reinforce the SPVs.

Because most companies will elect financial success as their primary strong performance value, their secondary performance values may be the qualitative ways to attain financial success. The SPVs must be communicated clearly and in detail so that the key leader's immediate lieutenants understand them. Documenting them in writing is helpful. Establishing the SPVs, then, is the first step toward designing a good reward plan and ensuring good performance.

Operationalizing the strong performance values of the company requires a business plan. Sound short- and long-term planning has always been a characteristic of successful companies. Good business plans include administrative strategies for technology, manufacturing, human relations, finance, and community affairs. The plans extend the strong performance values of the key leader throughout the organization and make them both meaningful and measurable. A good business plan considers the strengths and weaknesses of the company and its competitors. It outlines how the organization can respond to its business environment in an effective manner and remain flexible in its responses to external changes. Contingencies are allowed and planned for, and the possibility of surprises is minimized as much as possible.

The planning objective is to identify not only what is to be done but how it should be done and who should do it. All roles are identified and communicated. Tactical plans are established for the operational units of the company. The business plan describes how the results are to be achieved. The key leader and his or her chief executives should make up the cadre who communicate the specifics of the plan.

To integrate the business plan and the SPVs thoroughly, management compensation objectives that define the role financial rewards will play in reinforcing and communicating the key leader's strong performance values in the plan must be set. Objective setting requires that two series of questions concerning the business be answered. The first set of questions may include the following:

1. What criteria will best associate the interests of the shareholders with those of the manager?
2. In what technology and market areas does the company now have a significant advantage? Where are the company's strongest competitors? Where is it reasonable to expect the company could gain an advantage?
3. Are there any gaps in the high technology market the company could fill?
4. Is a plan of leading or following technology best for the company? Why?
5. What product or service areas should be emphasized in the short term? Are these the same ones that should be emphasized in the longer term? If not, which areas should be stressed in the long term?
6. Should the company diversify or emphasize a more narrow line of products? How should this be accomplished?
7. Of the technological opportunities available to the company, which should receive the most capital investment? Which should have second and third priority?

These and other questions help the company define its business plan. The next set of questions links the objectives of the compensation program with the objectives of the business plan. The set of management compensation questions must include the following:

1. What should be the mix between base salaries and short-term and long-term incentives? Is this emphasis consistent with the business plans? Why?
2. What specific qualitative (SPV) milestones can be assigned to each functional area? How should they be tied to the incentive plans?
3. What specific incentive plan can reward group efforts toward the achievement of an identified SPV?
4. Of all the measures of improvement in corporate worth that are available, which will best measure the performance of this specific company given its current financial situation? For example, should performance improvements be measured in terms of how the company compares to its business competitors?

The answers to these and other questions help to shape the company's incentive compensation objectives. Once finalized, the objectives identify the parameters of the management compensation program. Armed with management compensation objectives, executives can outline and evaluate alternate incentive plan designs. They can weigh the advantages and disadvantages of each plan. In some cases, executives simulate plans to ascertain which approach best communicates and reinforces desired management behavior. Once the best alternative is identified, the design, implementation, and communication phases are undertaken. In these phases, eligibility requirements, quantitative and qualitative performance criteria, and administrative procedures are established.

Once a plan has been implemented, the key leader should establish procedures that will ensure the plan remains consistent with the SPVC and compensation objectives of the organization. A periodic audit of the plan is necessary to determine whether it requires any modification to keep it in line with the organization's values and objectives.

Example of an Incentive Plan

Because the attainment of strong performance values can be ascertained only after the performance period is over, milestones that identify incremental success must be set. Short-term incentive plans recognize that these milestones have been met. Thus, they serve to communicate the importance of attaining the SPVs and reward performance that is directed toward their attainment.

This section of the chapter presents a simplified example of how a short-term incentive plan can be developed. When the financial SPV is identified as the principal objective that will result from the attainment of all other SPVs, the first step in the development of the incentive plan is to define the organization's financial SPV for the year.

Earnings per share, return on sales, and net pretax profit are the important indicators of the financial SPV. In this example, these three indicators, which represent the primary SPV, make up 60 percent of a manager's incentive for a year. For the sake of simplicity, each SPV is worth 20 percent. The other SPVs make up the other 40 percent of the manager's incentive.

If the company achieves all of its SPVs for the year, the manager receives 50 percent of base salary as an incentive award. The manager can receive as little as 2 percent of base salary if he or she makes 70 percent of fully satisfactory performance on only one SPV. If the manager misses 70 percent of goal on all SPVs, no award is made. The most the manager can receive is 75 percent of base salary even if he or she exceeds the maximum performance level on all SPVs.

Table 5-1 shows what percentage of base salary a manager will receive as incentive when 70, 100, or 125 percent of each primary SPV is attained. According to table 5-1, if a manager makes $60,000 per year in base salary and attains all three SPVs, the manager will receive 30 percent of base, or $18,000 (30 percent × $60,000 = $18,000). If the manager attains 70 percent of target for each part of the profit SPV, the manager will receive 2 percent of base salary for each SPV, or a total of 6 percent, or $3,600 (6 percent × $60,000 = $3,600). If the manager exceeds 125 percent of target for each part of the SPV the manager will receive 45 percent of base salary, or $27,000 (45 percent × $60,000 = $27,000). Remember, the manager cannot get more than 75 percent of base salary from the entire incentive plan.

Table 5-1
Quantitative Strong Performance Values

	Percent of Target Attained	Percent of Base as Incentive
Earnings per share	70%	2%
	100%	10%
	125% or more	15%
Return on sales	70%	2%
	100%	10%
	125% or more	15%
Net pretax profit	70%	2%
	100%	10%
	125% or more	15%

Table 5-2
Qualitative Strong Performance Values

	Percent of Target Attained	Percent of Base as Incentive
Technical excellence	70%	2%
	100%	7.5%
	125%	11.25%
Competitive advantage	70%	2%
	100%	7.5%
	125%	11.25%
Community responsibilities	70%	2%
	100%	5%
	125%	7.5%

In this example, in addition to the primary financial SPV, the company is attempting to achieve three secondary SPVs: technical excellence, competitive advantage, and community responsibilities. In reality, all three SPVs would be described in detail. To keep this example brief, however, the descriptions have been omitted here. If all objectives are obtained, the manager will receive another 20 percent of base salary as an incentive award. The weighting of the three secondary (or qualitative) SPVs is given in table 5-2.

Table 5-3 shows how a sample manager would be awarded with this plan. If the manager earns $60,000 a year, according to table 5-3, the manager would receive an annual incentive of 47.5 percent of base salary or $28,500 (47.5 percent × $60,000 = $28,500). The manager exceeded the annual SPV objectives in two areas (earnings per share and return on sales),

Table 5-3
Sample Incentive Plan Computation

Strong Performance Value	Weight	Percent of Base at Target	Actual Performance	Percent of Base Award
Earnings per share	20%	10%	130%	15%
Return on sales	20%	10%	125%	15%
Net pretax profit	20%	10%	100%	10%
Technical excellence	15%	7.5%	100%	7.5%
Competitive advantage	15%	7.5%	45%	0%
Community responsibilities	10%	5%	40%	0%
	100%	50%		47.5%

made the objectives in two areas (net pretax profit and technical excellence), and missed the minimum threshold in two areas (competitive advantage and community responsibilities).

This is a very simple example, but it shows how SPVs can be used in short-term incentive plans. It also shows that nonfinancial SPVs, such as technical excellence, are subjective and must be described. Their descriptions should be communicated to managers periodically throughout the year to reinforce them and make sure they are well understood.

Trends in Short-Term Plans

Key leaders in the most successful high technology companies are combining qualitative and quantitative strong performance values in their incentive plans. They are, as a result, communicating more closely with their managers on the matters that are essential to the continuous good performance of their companies. They expend the necessary time in managing the communications of their SPVs and ensuring that their short-term incentive plans continue to work effectively.

The major trend in short-term incentive planning is the utilization of financial criteria that communicate to both the financial world and internal managers the importance of profit performance and descriptive criteria that show managers how to attain the performance values of the company. In short, the trend among good corporate performers is to integrate culture and administrative systems more closely.

Summary

Managers in the SPVC companies are participating in annual incentive plans that help sustain the cultures of their companies. Companies are designing their incentive plans as communications tools to improve profit performance and emphasize cooperative teamwork. Although the individual is still recognized as essential to success, most high technology companies are rewarding individuals for their contributions to successful group performance.

6

Management
Long-Term Incentives

In order for managers to identify with their company's culture, the interests of the manager and the organization must be intertwined in some way. Well-designed short-term incentive plans that grant significant financial rewards to performance that contributes to the attainment of the strong performance values of the company accomplish this to some extent. Good base salaries contribute to the intertwining too. Associating performance in the short-term with the company's longer-range plans for the attainment of its performance values also helps to integrate the interests of the manager with the company's interests. This requires that the company use financial reward systems that measure performance over a period of more than a year.

The best long-term incentive plans award the performance of a manager in a way that makes the manager feel more like an owner than an employee of the company. Such plans are closely tied to corporate culture. Compensation-plan designers who want the program design to match company culture must start with an available long-term incentive compensation vehicle and adapt it so that it will communicate the specific SPVs of their culture. The tinkerers of long-term incentive plans aim to spend their incentive dollars in a way that gets the best performance and the most identification with the culture as possible.

Management Incentive Practices

Once established, a strong performance value culture must be maintained and supported. The key leader must continually seek and evaluate opportunities to do this. Long-term incentive plans financially reward the continuing successful performance of the management team members who help the key leader sustain the company culture. Because these incentive plans measure managers' performance over a period of more than a year (usually from three to five years), managers are encouraged to look to the future and ensure that their current actions reflect the most desirable long-range performance.

Well-designed long-term management incentive plans associate the financial well-being of the managers with that of the stockholders so that, when the company makes money for the investors, the managers also benefit financially. This linking of management and shareholder interests can be accomplished best if managers' attention is directed to the company's long-term and short-term business objectives. These objectives, which embody the company's SPVs, must become intrinsically important to managers. Top management and the stockholders, therefore, must be willing to reward managers for making the company run profitably. Being given the opportunity to share in the financial future of the company is a very important incentive and one reason managers come to identify with the company. Managers gain both extrinsically and intrinsically from equity ownership. Acquiring a piece of the company is the best way for managers to capitalize on their management talents. Sharing the financial performance of the company with those managers who made a measurable difference in the long run serves to reinforce the company's values because, by creating a class of employees identified as manager-owners, the company is showing the managers who want to be more than employees, who want to receive more than a salary and an annual cash bonus, that consistent high-quality performance in accord with the company's objectives will get them what they want.

Stock and Nonstock Plans

The most popular long-term incentive plan is the one that offers a stock option. Such a plan provides managers with a contingent opportunity to purchase stock and gain from stock appreciation. Stock option plans usually are supplemented by plans that pay off in cash at the end of the performance period. The resultant total program depends in part on the price of the common stock of the company, but also rewards outstanding employee performance with cash.

For years, stock has been the principal device by which executives have accumulated capital. In recent years, key leaders have begun to worry that the price of common stock will not continue to rise as much as it has in the past and, therefore, may not provide new managers with the opportunity to build an estate. Stock price must move up for a stock option plan to be worthwhile. Managers must feel ownership is worth something if ownership is to serve as an incentive to perform well and a reason to stay with the company.

Stock can be used by a company as an offensive weapon to attract good people and as a defensive weapon to keep good people. All companies use their stock and stock-option plans to attract important managers from other companies. If a manager is recruited by a company with a greater potential for common stock growth, the manager may leave his or her current employer. This makes it critical for companies to develop programs that do not depend on stock options as the sole reward for management performance. Another reason for creating a nonstock incentive plan is that sometimes management performance does not directly affect the long-term price of common stock.

A primary concern in the development of nonstock compensation is the selection of financial and nonfinancial criteria to be used to measure management performance. The plan must be based on clear and relevant criteria that the managers view as important to both management and the company. In most cases, this requires the company to use both qualitative and quantitative criteria to measure performance aimed at achieving a final financial objective. The qualitative criteria identify the management deeds necessary for the attainment of the final financial result that is to be shared with managers.

The available accounting methods and other factors may influence how accurately financial performance is measured and reported. Sometimes high technology companies must move quickly to take advantage of a business opportunity, and some of the ways leaders raise capital or transfer funds from one segment of the company to another may upset the financial picture for a while, although such strategic actions may be essential to the long-term success of the company. Because such events and accounting methods may skew financial measures of performance, much attention has been focused on developing nonfinancial measures of corporate performance.

Venture Capital and Incentives

Venture capital is essential to the development of high technology. Providers of venture capital do not want their stock ownership positions to be diluted. The major shareholders in closely held high technology companies feel the same way. An owner who has taken risks to get a company going wants to retain control of it. The more common stock issued, the weaker becomes current owners' ownership positions. However, unless a company can offer its valuable managers an equity position, it may not be able to keep its quality management team. On the one hand, managers want to be given the opportunity to own stock; on the other hand, current owners want to retain company ownership. Top executives must recognize both objectives to keep company performance high.

A few principal owners are interested only in increasing the worth of their companies so they can attract the best price if and when they want to merge or sell. These owners are not interested in solving management compensation problems, and so little can be done to develop effective compensation plans in these companies. Such single-purpose owners are in the minority, however. Most owners are trying to deal with the problems that rewarding management performance without weakening ownership positions pose.

Compared to the companies whose stock is widely held, closely held organizations may encounter more serious problems if their management-compensation plans offer stock options. Although these problems can be solved, the companies will not be able to address them adequately without involving the managers who sustain the financial health of the company. Some owners do not enlist the aid of their professional management team because they are afraid that involving their managers may increase managers' expectations. These high technology companies tend to pay higher base salaries and award larger incentives, but the managers do not tend to identify strongly with company practices. Most managers will not feel a part of a culture in which they do not have a share and an active role.

Types of Long-Term Incentives

A variety of long-term programs exist in high technology companies. All have at their foundations several basic plans. Key leaders have found that some combination of incentive plans creates the best compensation strategy. The most successful companies adapt the standard plans to their specific needs.

The effective compensation planner is always ready to take advantage of a new design opportunity. Tax and accounting changes have encouraged plan designers to keep a flexible posture. The design and prevalence of stock-related incentive plans has changed in response to modifications in tax laws. Tax law changes were influential in the shift from using qualified stock options to using nonqualified stock options, in the use of stock appreciation rights, and in the use of incentive stock options in incentive plans. These changes will continue to affect how incentive plans are designed.

Stock Option Plans

Because the qualified stock option plan lost its tax advantages a few years ago, the foundation stock option plan is nonqualified, allowing the rewarded employee the right to buy a stipulated number of shares of common stock at an established price over a specific period of time. The time period of the option usually is ten years, although some high technology companies offer other time periods.

Although most companies do not do this, a company may grant a stock option at a price below the fair market value of the stock at the time of award. Most options have vesting requirements of some kind that must be met. Many plans provide that some common stock acquired under a previously granted stock option may be used to pay for at least part of the stock available under a newly granted nonqualified stock option. All high technology companies require that option plans be approved by shareholders before they become effective.

At the time of award, nonqualified stock options have no federal income tax consequences. When the options are exercised, the excess of the market value of the stock over the option price of the stock is taxed as ordinary income. Any appreciation the manager experiences in the value of the stock from the date the stock option is exercised to the date the stock is sold is treated as a long-term capital gain, assuming the manager has held the shares for longer than one year. The company receives a tax deduction when an employee realizes ordinary income in an amount equal to the employee's tax obligation.

The company incurs no accounting expense if the option price and the market value of the stock are the same at the date the options are granted. However, as was suggested earlier, dilution of the number of shares outstanding may occur, and this would be reflected in the company's earnings-per-share calculation. A nonqualified stock option plan also may be developed using formula-related stock (for example, book value shares) instead of publicly traded stock.

Stock Appreciation Rights

Key leaders in high technology companies usually use stock appreciation rights (SARs) to minimize the tax burdens resulting from the awarding of nonqualified stock options. Although SARs can be granted alone, the high technology companies that use SARs grant them with nonqualified stock options. The manager pays nothing for the stock appreciation rights and, in most instances, can exercise the rights when the tax obligations from exercising the options are incurred. The rights appreciate as the attendant shares of stock appreciate, but, in most of the companies that use the rights, appreciation is limited to 50 or 60 percent of the growth in the value of the stock options with which the SARs are associated. Although most companies pay the awards in cash, some pay in common stock. All plans require shareholder approval at the same time the nonqualified stock option plan is approved.

The rights do not incur a tax obligation when they are granted. When they are exercised, the amount received becomes taxable to the employee at ordinary income rates. The company takes a tax deduction equal to the employee's ordinary income tax obligation. From an accounting standpoint, estimated expense is accrued quarterly from the date of grant to the date of exercise and usually is equal to the appreciation during the year.

Incentive Stock Options

ISOs returned to incentive plans most of the tax advantages that the departed qualified stock options had offered. The ISO provides the manager with a right to purchase common stock (at a price not less than fair market value on the date of award) for a specific period of time. The option must be granted within ten years of shareholder approval or adoption, whichever is earlier. The manager must exercise the options within ten years of grant, and the options must be exercised in the sequence in which they were granted. The maximum grant per employee is limited to $100,000 of stock as of the date of grant. Stock acquired under a previously granted option can be used to pay for the exercise of ISOs. Stockholder approval is necessary within twelve months (before or after) of the plan's adoption.

The important advantage of an incentive stock option is that the recipient does not receive taxable income at the time of grant or exercise. Any appreciation in value from exercise to sale is taxed as a long-term capital gain if the shares are held for at least one year from the date of exercise and two years from the date they were granted. The company does not receive a tax deduction from incuring a business expense as a result of granting ISOs, and some leaders in this book's research sample felt that this was a reason to limit the use of ISOs in their long-term incentive programs. ISOs do not incur accounting expense upon either grant or exercise, but they may have a dilutent effect on earnings per share.

The Tax Equity and Fiscal Responsibility Act (TEFRA) of 1982 changed the taxation of ISOs. The effective tax rate now varies between 20 and 40 percent, depending on the magnitude of growth in stock price and other taxable income at the time of exercise.

Many companies use ISOs in combination with nonqualified stock options when they want to grant a manager an option award in excess of $100,000. High technology companies prefer to use these options as much as possible, especially as new grants, because ISOs help the value of their managers' awards to catch up with the appreciation in stock value that employees in other companies are experiencing.

Restricted Stock Plans

Restricted stock plans are receiving much attention from key leaders in the companies with SPVCs. With such a plan, common stock is issued, subject to restrictions, at no cost to the employee and at full market value. The stock becomes available to the manager as he or she meets the restrictions. In most cases, in addition to the accomplishment of a series of performance objectives important to the long-term performance of the company, a waiting period is required. The manager has contingent ownership of the stock until the restrictions are satisfied and usually is paid dividend equivalents. All companies obtain stockholder approval before adopting a restricted stock plan.

The manager receives no taxable income from the stock while the restrictions are in effect. When the restrictions are satisfied, the excess of fair market value over the employee's cost is taxable as ordinary income. If the manager so wishes, he or she may elect, within thirty days of award, to be taxed on the value of the stock (at the time of award) over the employee cost. Subsequent appreciation in excess of fair market value is taxed as long-term capital gain, assuming the stock is held for over one year. Dividends are taxed at ordinary rates unless early tax payment is made. If the stock is forfeited because the restrictions are not met, no deductible loss can be claimed by the employee.

The company takes a tax deduction in the amount and at the time the employee is taxed at ordinary rates. Estimated expense is accrued annually in an amount equal to the difference between the stock's market value on the date of grant and the price paid by the employee, if the manager pays anything for the stock. If forfeited, the recorded compensation expense may be reversed to reflect the forfeiture. Dividends paid are not charged against income.

This type of reward, when used in combination with incentive stock options, provides companies with some interesting opportunities to combine stock ownership with qualitative performance criteria. These design alternatives for incentive programs are very attractive to the high technology tinkerers.

Phantom Stock Plans

Phantom stock plans are often used when common stock dilution is a problem or when companies are closely held but the stock price provides some opportunity for gain. With this type of plan, managers are awarded units that represent, not an actual ownership in the company, but a specific number of shares of stock. When the units mature, they usually are equal to the value of actual common shares of stock. The award may reflect either the value of the common shares or the appreciation in the value of the stock.

In high technology companies, such plans usually are designed to reflect the worth of common stock. At the time the units mature, the plan can pay their value in cash or in stock. In most high technology companies, cash is awarded. The manager receives no taxable income when phantom shares are awarded. When the units mature and the plan pays their value, the cash is taxed as ordinary income. The company takes a tax deduction at the time the manager realizes the ordinary income. Expense is accrued quarterly by amortizing the initial value of the awards and/or appreciation over the period of the plan.

Performance Share/Unit Plans

Internal measures of corporate performance are used in the performance share/unit plan. Many key leaders are trying to develop this type of plan into a usable supplement to stock options. The challenge in such development is selecting appropriate qualitative and quantitative performance criteria—criteria that are consistent with the SPVs of the company.

Awards in units are granted, with no employee cost, for a specified period. They are earned as performance criteria are satisfied. Awards are supposed to be associated directly with the achievement of goals and objectives over a period of time, usually from three to five years. Awards may be made sequentially over a period of years (plans that grant such awards are known as sequential award plans). Different performance criteria may be used for each period. The plan may introduce both quantitative and qualitative criteria that reflect the SPVs, business plans, and tactics of the company.

No taxable income is realized until the award is paid. If the award is made in stock, subsequent appreciation is taxed as a long-term capital gain if the shares are held for over one year. The company may take a tax deduction in the amount of ordinary income. Estimated expense is accrued quarterly by amortizing the initial value of the awards and subsequent appreciation over the period the award is earned.

This plan is very flexible, and high technology companies use it to supplement nearly all other compensation devices. The plan offers a good opportunity for design creativity because it depends on the development of credible performance criteria.

Junior Stock Plans

Junior stock plans are often used when the company is still in the venture-capital stage of development. The method also may be attractive to companies whose risk-reward ratios are high. A junior stock award allows the manager to purchase a separate class of stock at a stipulated price. The award is vested in the manager (or the manager earns the award) if the company achieves certain specified performance goals. Thus, the plan relates the grant to performance values. In concept, a junior-stock plan is relatively straightforward.

Junior stocks make up a special separate class of shares that are issued with less attractive rights than common shares. Because these shares have substantially less value in terms of their company liquidation, voting, and dividend rights, they are offered to managers at a discount well below the fair market value of common shares. The risks and uncertainty associated with achieving performance goals are another reason junior shares are priced well below common shares. Managers may convert their junior shares into common shares on a one-to-one ratio (or alternative ratio) by making specific and identified contributions to the achievement of company performance goals. For example, conversion might be triggered by the attainment of X dollars of cumulative profits over a three-year performance period. Performance goals also may be relative; for example, conversion may depend on the company's outperforming peer companies or beating industry norms.

Upon conversion (triggered by the achievement of goals) junior shares are exchanged for common shares on a tax-free basis. If the election offered by Section 83(b) is taken, the appreciation in the common stock since the date of grant is taxed at the rate of capital gains (maximum of 20 percent). This, of course, is the principal reason managers find this plan attractive. The company, however, receives no corresponding tax deduction.

Junior stock plans may have vesting requirements in addition to performance requirements. Companies typically reserve the right to repurchase shares upon managers' termination of employment. Repurchase is made at the current fair market value or at the original purchase price, whichever is lower.

To explain how junior stock plans work, an example is presented here. Assume that a manager has purchased junior shares at their current market value of ten dollars. An independent financial advisor has determined that, given the performance requirements built into the junior shares, ten dollars is the market value of the shares. Because the manager has paid the true market value, there is no tax due on the purchase. If the manager so elects, according to Section 83(b), the ten-dollar figure will be the cost basis for future tax purposes.

If the manager achieves the stipulated performance requirements, he or she may convert the junior stock into shares of common stock. This conversion takes place on a tax-free basis because the manager is exchanging one type of the company's security for another. At the sale of the stock, taxes will be due on the difference between the current market price and the original market price of the junior stock (assuming the manager so elected, the difference will be taxed at the capital-gains rate).

Thus, if the manager sells the common shares at their market value of seventy-five dollars, he or she will be taxed thirteen dollars ($75 − $10 × 20 percent capital gains tax = $13). The total cost to the manager is the initial cost of the junior stock plus the tax incurred on the sale of the common shares ($10 + $13 = $23). The net gain to the executive, then, equals the money earned from the sale of the common shares at market value minus the initial cost of the junior stock and the tax on the sale ($75 − $23 = $52).

If the plan can be integrated fully with the organization's strong performance values, a company should include the plan in its incentive program. However, junior stock plans should not be used if their only attraction lies in the tax advantage they offer recipients.

Incentives to Sustain Performance Values

The strong performance values of a high technology company will not be reflected in its long-term incentive program if the company has only one measure of performance or a single approach to long-term compensation. To ensure that the strong performance values of the company are well and consistently communicated by the incentive/compensation program, the company must use several plans and integrate them with short-term incentive plans.

The performance criteria used in the plans not only must reflect the firm's SPVs but also must associate the interests of the managers with those of the shareholders. The stockholders are interested in the company as an investment; the managers are interested in the company as an environment where they can apply their trade and be rewarded for their contributions. If the company does not measure up to its established performance goals, both shareholders and managers are frustrated.

The tough-luck school of management incentive planning says that it is unfortunate the company did not do well when the manager performed so well. The wait-a-minute school says that the manager has only to go to a company that is better able to recognize the successful performance of individuals or groups. Neither school addresses high technology companies' needs. High technology managers are an attractive and mobile commodity. Unless managment incentive plans are well designed for the longer term, a manager may stay with one company as long as its stock is going up and then join another company that offers better stock opportunities. Losing valuable managers can have detrimental effects on a company's performance. A competitive incentive plan that communicates the company's strong performance values benefits both valuable employees and the company. In addition, such a plan may help the company to acquire new employees and to indicate career paths for upward mobility within the organization. An incentive plan that contributes to good corporate performance also helps to satisfy the needs of that company's shareholders.

Incentive Plan Participation

Incentive-plan participation can be determined after the plan is designed. The managers who have the most impact on the criteria used to measure the company's success are key candidates. However, plan participation should be based on job content—not the incumbent or job title. Some managers may not hold jobs that make meaningful contributions to the attainment of company performance values.

Exclusion or inclusion in long-term incentive plans may vary from year to year, depending on what the company is trying to achieve. If the abilities required by a job are identified as necessary for the achievement of the objectives tied to the long-range compensation plan, the job will be included. It is what the manager does, whether his or her job would help meet the objectives to be reinforced by the compensation plan, that determines eligibility for the plan. When participation can be explained in terms of the specific tasks or goals to be accomplished, selecting participants is easy.

Incentive Performance Criteria

The period during which manager performance is measured varies from company to company and within a company, depending on how long accomplishing the business goal or objective is expected to take. In the companies with strong performance value cultures the period is seldom longer than three years. The long-term plan may have more than one performance period; one period may be scheduled to end after two years, another after three, and a third after five years. Short-term incentive plans take care of incremental achievements, and the special award program may be used to reward unexpected contributions.

Because performance values are specific to an organization and its key leader, the award periods must be significant in terms of the company's objectives; periods need not reflect other companies' time frames. Business does not always work on the three-year cycle, especially in the high technology field, and so long-term performance periods should be flexible.

Leaders may not always be satisfied with the financial criteria used to measure managers' long-term performance in the company. As a result, criteria may be changed periodically to reflect changing expectations. Qualitative milestones that are relevant to sales, engineering, personnel, finance, manufacturing, and other job families or organizational units should be selected as part of the measurement criteria.

To ensure that the entire organization will succeed in the long-term, rather than just reinforce the good performance of parts of the company, the best corporate performers emphasize group performance in their long-term incentive plans. When organizations are growing quickly, as are most high technology companies, working well as a team is more important than individual performance because management staff generally is lean and managers' duties may vary. Until the individual's contribution can be defined clearly and becomes static, rewarding team work is the key leader's best bet. Plans that emphasize group performance often use multiple criteria to measure individuals' contributions to team success.

Incentive Award Size

The financial rewards of long-term plans must appear (to managers) worth staying with the company to earn. Successful high technology companies use programs that give managers the opportunity to earn long-term compensation equivalent to about 20 percent of base salary for each year of the plan. In other words, a program that runs for three years could provide the manager with an award equal to about 60 percent of base salary.

Most plans provide a lower limit of about 10 percent of base salary per year. Few companies make awards below this level because they want the managers to view the awards as worthwhile. On the other hand, only a very few programs provide managers with the opportunity to accumulate financial equity that is equal to more than 20 percent of base salary per year. Larger capital accumulation tends to be the result of appreciation in the value of the managers' common stock during the period of the long-term plan.

Management Benefits and Perquisites

Although high technology companies offer extra management benefits and perquisites, few key leaders view them as essential incentives for managers to sustain performance that is consistent with the SPVs. Some key leaders believe that indirect compensation plans cause more confusion than they are worth. However, because they are a part of total management compensation programs, the most common plans will be discussed here.

A number of high technology companies offer additional benefits only to managers. In most cases, the plans are designed to replace a larger proportion of a manager's income than would be replaced by the company's general retirement vehicle. The plans usually are based on the employee's total cash compensation rather than just base salary, on which most other retirement plans are based. The plans seldom have vesting and funding rules. The company contribution is tax deductible, and the money increases tax free in a trust until payments begin at the time of retirement.

Most companies offer group term life insurance as a death benefit. Managers often are covered by the same formula that applies to all other employees, unless extra life insurance is provided. The practice varies in high technology companies, but smaller firms rarely provide as much life insurance as do larger companies in the industry. All companies provide supplemental medical benefits to their management group. These benefits often make up for any unpaid amounts under the company's regular health plans.

Some companies offer variable benefit plans. The plans allow managers to choose among a number of extra benefits or perquisites. The key leaders of high technology organizations have expressed interest in this type of plan because it can meet managers' needs without incurring great costs to the company. By offering a group of benefits that do not generate income to the employee or are entitled to a statutory exclusion from taxation, a company can contain the costs of benefits. Such benefits may include: first-class air travel; reimbursement for home business entertainment; liberal expense accounts; access to an executive dining room, custom offices, and/or reserved parking places; insured medical-expense reimbursement; premiums on the first $50,000 of group term life insurance; and, under certain circumstances, interest-free loans.

Key leaders in high technology companies are interested in these plans principally because they are interested in any opportunity to improve the design of their job-evaluation, pay-administration, and short- and long-term incentive plans. In general, the leaders of the more successful companies believe that compensation money must be directed to base salary or incentive/compensation plans rather than to benefit plans. These leaders do not think that management benefits serve as communications channels or provide for better management identification with SPVs. Variable benefits are viewed as an exception, because executives see them as an important cost containment trend in compensation plan design.

Management Incentive Objectives

Some long-term plans are better suited to the objectives of a specific company than are others. The challenge facing the plan designer is selecting the alternatives that best reflect the strong performance values of the organization. In addition, because certain compensation programs offer tax benefits to the manager and/or the company, the incentive plan designer may want to consider including them in the complete incentive program.

Table 6-1 outlines the possible features of each long-term incentive plan. A score of *A* indicates that the plan may be designed to reflect the feature listed in the left column very well. A score of *B* means the plan provides only moderate design opportunity to reflect a feature, and a score of *C* indicates that the plan may not be designed to reflect the feature. Basic plans are only the foundation of an organizationally appropriate program, and how well they are used in the overall design is subject to the creativity of the program designer.

As table 6-1 shows, the stock option plan measures the performance of a company in terms of the price of its stock, as does an incentive stock option. By obtaining the shares, the manager has the same opportunity to gain that other shareholders have. In addition, the stock option and ISO plans offer possible tax advantages to the manager. However, because the plans' performance measure is the price of the company's common stock, they do not give the designer the measurement flexibility that other incentive plans may offer.

The best corporate performers offer stock options and ISOs because they want their managers to own company stock and because they believe the price of the company's stock is a good measure of company performance. The use of these options is popular with the managers because it offers them the opportunity to earn a piece of the action. No other long-term incentive alternative has the intrinsic value to the manager that the stock option and ISO plans have. Much of their value lies in the fact that they offer an ownership position. Even when the stock price seems to fail to reflect the company's performance, offering ownership communicates to the manager his or her importance to the company. Options play an important role in linking the performance of the company with that of the manager.

Stock appreciation rights are used principally with stock options to help the manager meet the financial obligations associated with exercising the options. Also, the SARs serve to defray the tax consequences of stock options. Because the stock appreciation right is granted to help the manager finance the stock options, it does not directly support the SPVs of the company and cannot be used as a vehicle to measure company performance. The only message SARs communicate is that the company will help the manager pay for the stock options he or she has been awarded.

The restricted stock option plan provides that ownership of the stock is contingent upon the accomplishment of a series of hurdles or milestones. This type of program fits very well with the objectives of high technology companies with SPVCs. Like other stock option plans, the restricted stock option provides managers with the opportunity to attain an ownership posi-

Table 6–1
Rating Long-Term Incentive Plan Features

Plan Feature	Stock Option Plans	Stock Appreciation Rights	Incentive Stock Options	Restricted Stock Options	Phantom Stock Plans	Performance Share/ Unit Plans
Measures appreciation in price of common stock	A	A	A	A	A	C
Measures performance criteria in addition to common stock performance	C	C	C	A	C	A
Provides considerable design flexibility to reflect SPVs	B	B	B	A	B	A
Requires investment by the manager	A	C	A	B	C	C
Requires no investment by the manager	C	A	C	B	A	A
Involves management ownership in the company	A	C	A	A	C	C
May offer tax/accounting advantages to manager or company	A	C	A	A	C	C
Is utilized by high technology companies that perform well	A	C	A	A	C	A

tion, it measures company performance in terms of the price of common stock, and may offer tax advantages. Unlike other options, the restricted stock option offers the incentive plan designer considerable flexibility.

The price of common stock is used as the corporate performance measure in the phantom stock plan, also. With this plan, no stock or stock options are granted, and the manager makes no investment. The worth of the incentive increases or decreases with the price of the stock. At the end of a specific period, the manager receives the cash value of any appreciation in stock multiplied by the number of phantom stock options received. For example, if a manager receives one hundred phantom stock options that can be exercised after three years, and the stock goes up $500 in the three years, the manager receives $50,000 (100 × $500 = $50,000). If the stock goes down, the manager receives nothing.

The companies that perform well tend to use other long-term incentive plans more than they use the phantom stock plan because the key leaders prefer to use both financial and nonfinancial performance measures. Since most already use stock options, which they believe more closely associate the interests of the manager with those of the shareholder because they require investment by the manager, the key leaders want the other plans in their incentive programs to incorporate qualitative criteria.

The performance share/unit plan can be designed to reflect a variety of SPVs. Because of this, share/unit plans are used often by successful high technology companies. The plan allows for the use of all manner of criteria and time periods. Its only creative boundaries are the incentive objectives of the key leader and how those objectives fit within the culture of the company. This type of plan can be designed to pay off in either stock or cash, and it is the only long-term incentive plan that can be applied at the small-group level. Key leaders prefer this type of plan because of its flexibility, which permits them to use the plan as a supplement to the stock option and/or restricted stock option plan.

Steps to Incentive Plan Design

Once the long-term incentive objectives have been established, the appropriate program may be selected and developed.

The designers of a long-term incentive program must begin by documenting the specific strong performance values of the company. Once this has been accomplished, the designers must determine how the key leader will measure performance against the values; that is, what criteria will be used to measure whether the values have been attained in the longer term. In addition, time periods must be identified. Some suggest a three- or four-year measurement period, while others recommend longer intervals. At the end of this design process, the following will have been accomplished:

1. Strong performance values defined.
2. Specific qualitative and quantitative criteria selected.
3. Managers whose jobs can impact the SPVs identified.
4. Time periods over which performance will be measured established.
5. Methods for integrating long- and short-term incentive plans determined.

When all this has been accomplished, designers will be able to select the combination of incentive plans that best meets the objectives and expectations of both management and the key leader.

Incentive Example

To further explain how an incentive program is developed, an example, which necessarily is too general in order to clarify a point or two, is presented here. Assume that plan designers have developed the following long-term incentive objectives that reflect the strong performance values of the company's key leader:

1. Profit performance, as reflected by common stock performance (quantitative), improved return on sales (quantitative), and improved cash flow (quantitative).
2. Technical excellence, as measured by reduction in quality rejects (qualitative) and progress toward improvement of XYZ products (qualitative). (Both measurements must be stated in specific terms.)
3. Competitive advantage, as measured by improved market penetration (quantitative) and a better prepared sales force (qualitative).

This company has only a very few managers without operational responsibilities and also has few middle managers. Its top two or three levels of management, then, have both broad and deep management responsibilities. Only members of the top three levels of management are identified as eligible for participation in long-term plans (although the short-term incentive plan is applied more broadly). In addition, because management believes it can forecast only three years in the future, the long-term performance period is set at three years. Short-term plans will be used to reward small-group SPVs, while the long-term program will measure corporate performance as a whole. (This structure would be too simple in practice, but it will give a general idea of the plan design.)

Given these determinations, the long-term incentive program could include the following elements:

1. Stock options (and ISOs) to measure common stock performance and provide equity in company.
2. Restricted stock options that emphasize technical performance and include qualitative yardsticks, such as reduction in quality rejects, as well as measure stock performance and provide an earned equity position.
3. Performance share/unit plan that includes the quantitative criteria of profit performance (improved return on sales and cash flow) and the qualitative criteria of competitive advantage (market penetration and sales force improvement).

This program would provide the key leader with a multiple-feature program that reflects a number of strong performance values. The program does not depend on only one element for appreciation, and it uses a wide range of criteria that communicate the importance of performance that is consistent with the SPVs of the company.

Trends in Long-Term Plans

In the future, earning a long-term incentive award will be more difficult. More and more companies are emphasizing the accomplishment of objectives that are consistent with the strong performance values of the company. Managers are being rewarded for helping the key leader effectively communicate the SPVs, for supporting the high performance of the culture, and for ensuring that the company culture, which emphasizes SPVs, is sustained. In other words, the long-term plans are geared toward continuity of management, performance, and leadership. To earn a long-term incentive award, a manager must actually contribute to the attainment of SPVs over the long term.

Summary

Companies that consistently outperform their competitors satisfy the needs of their venture capitalists, shareholders, executives, and managers. These companies have sustained strong performance values that permeate their cultures. To help the key leaders communicate the SPVs, the companies use administrative systems such as long-range incentive plans that provide managers who perform in accord with the company's strong performance values with both intrinsic and extrinsic rewards. The intrinsic rewards result from being productive members of a successful team. Extrinsic rewards associate the financial well-being of the managers with that of the company.

What is necessary to obtain the rewards is communicated clearly in these most successful organizations. When a plan no longer helps one of these companies to communicate and reward behavior consistent with the SPVs, the company looks for a new approach. These organizations tinker with their long-term incentive plans to ensure that they always fit their corporate cultures.

7

A Close Look at the Companies that Perform the Best

The importance of establishing, maintaining, communicating, and reinforcing strong performance values to sustain excellent financial performance has been discussed already. In this chapter, the successful companies will be investigated as a group. How the management of organizational culture affects financial success; how corporate culture can be improved and changed; and the essential roles played by the leader, the strong performance values, the managers and other employees, and the administrative systems play will be reiterated. Also, the importance of staying flexible, trends in total management compensation, and how the best performers plan management-compensation activities and programs to emphasize SPVs will be explored.

The companies that perform well have much in common with the organizations that perform less satisfactorily. The one thing that is not common to both types of organizations is the existence of strong performance values. It is possible for companies to change their cultures, however, and adopt management by strong performance values. By doing this, the companies are likely to align themselves more closely with the group of successful SPV companies.

What Causes Very Good Financial Performance?

Everybody wants to know more about winners. Twenty-four of the companies investigated for this book outperformed the other companies in the study by a substantial margin. They sold more and made more money per sale. In addition, they were more prolific in their production of marketable technology. When measured by all quantitative and qualitative performance criteria, these companies consistently scored high. The fact that these companies make a lot more money than the other companies is a source of great satisfaction to their employees because they share in that financial success. Each of the companies has a winning culture, and the cooperation needed to keep it winning is communicated and reinforced regularly throughout the organization.

The cultures of the more successful organizations are distinguished from the cultures of poorer corporate performers by the existence of management by strong performance values. While some poor performers have strong cultures, they lack strong performance values. The values they do have may even be inhibiting their ability to perform well. To confirm the suggested impact of SPVs on performance, each of the twenty-four companies that excelled in the initial research were revisited by investigators. Investigators met at length with the key leaders of the companies and members of their senior management teams. In addition, they studied each organization in more detail to find out if any features other than SPVs consistently contributed to financial performance. The purpose of the return visits was to review, in detail, the accuracy of the conclusions reached after the initial phase of research and to make sure the information gathered earlier had been interpreted correctly. The hope was to identify what there was about these companies' cultures that contributed to their success and how (or whether) those factors could be applied in other organizations to help them improve their performance.

The additional information gathered during second visits will be valuable to executives in both the high technology industry and in other businesses. Although high technology companies served as the sample, the principles and examples uncovered by the study for this book can be used by companies in other industries to improve and sustain their good financial performance.

The second visits to the best corporate performers in the sample confirmed the investigators' initial conclusions. The main reason these companies performed better financially was their development of a strong performance value culture and their day-to-day use of strong performance values. The additional visits did not identify any other organizational or cultural variables that existed in all twenty-four companies and that had a consistent relationship with the sustained excellent financial performance of the organizations. In the homogeneous high technology industry, the culture that emphasizes doing well and the management effort that communicates the values of the culture on a continuing basis makes the difference when it comes to success.

Companies that Changed Their Cultures

The study for this book showed that the companies with cultures that openly emphasized performance and how to attain it did better than other companies. One of the most important questions that arose from the study results is whether the fundamental culture of a company can be modified within a reasonable time period. If it can, the next important question is how the change can be instituted. Because it has been shown that the best performers are those that manage by SPVs, the assumption is that a company that does not now manage by SPVs must begin to do so in order to perform better in the future.

Of the twenty-four successful companies investigated for this book, six were directed by key leaders who had been chief executive since their companies were founded. These leaders managed their companies with SPVs from the beginning. Because of this, these companies have not had to change their cultures to help them perform better financially.

Of the eighteen remaining companies in the sample group of companies that perform very well, seven were managed by executives who succeeded the original key leader and sustained the strong performance values and strong performance value culture the original leader established. These companies support the idea that an SPVC can be sustained by a well-designed management succession plan. They reinforce the importance of a cadre of executives who manage by SPVs and are groomed to assume the key leader's job.

However, the fact that a successor can sustain an existing culture does not provide information about the effects of changes of culture. To show that a company culture can be changed for the better, it must be demonstrated that the performance of a non-SPVC company can be improved either by a key leader who did not manage by SPVs but who begins to manage by SPVs and establishes an SPVC or by someone from outside the company who joins the company and introduces strong performance values.

The other eleven SPVC companies in the sample changed their cultures and improved their financial performance as the result of the introduction of management by SPVs either by a new key leader coming in from outside the company or by a new key leader promoted from within the company. In eight of the eleven companies, performance (as measured from a total financial perspective) had begun to improve within two years of the leadership change. In the other three companies, financial records were not available to the public for the period prior to the new key leaders' joining them because the companies went public at about the time the management changes were made. However, sales performance, adjusted for inflation, increased substantially in these three companies, which suggests that corporate culture can be changed for the better, with very desirable financial results.

The companies that experienced substantially improved financial performance after a management change that introduced an SPVC had either a weak or a mixed performance value culture before the leadership change. When the new key leader came from outside the corporation, the company usually had a weak performance value culture before the change. When the leader was promoted from within, the company usually had a mixed performance value culture before the change.

Starting Out with a Strong Performance Value Culture

When a company is managed by SPVs from its inception, the key leader's challenge is to sustain the culture. This requires the existence of a core group of operating executives who support the SPVC, who are prepared to succeed the key leader, and who manage the company in a manner consistent with the continuous communication and reinforcement of the strong performance values.

A key leader must groom the core group of executives as early in their management careers as possible. In most instances, the managers are with the company for a number of years before they become members of the core executive group. To groom managers for promotion, the key leader should spend as much time with them as possible to give them the opportunity to obtain a clear perspective of the strong performance values by working directly with the individual responsible for their development and communication. Extensive and prolonged personal contact between the key leader and his or her top management group is not present in the companies that perform less satisfactorily.

The management grooming process not only provides top executives who manage by SPVs to the company doing the grooming but also provides such executives to other companies. A key leader cannot assume that all of the managers who are learning to manage an organization by SPVs will stay with his or her company forever. Some of the managers will leave to take other jobs in different companies, and these become the leaders who transplant an SPVC from one company to another.

Because managers who have been groomed to lead by SPVs do occasionally join other organizations, a key leader must groom at least two or three extra well-qualified operating managers as potential members of the core executive group. This protects the company from cultural discontinuity. By making sure that they have a large enough supply of prepared managers, the key leaders will not be forced to replace one of the members of the core executive group with someone from outside the company who may not be able to help sustain the culture in the longer term.

Adopting a Strong Performance Value Culture

Many companies do not know how much difference having the right leader makes. Some of the companies visited during the investigation for this book had very strong leaders and even strong organizational cultures, but they were not among the group of good performers. Although many of the executives seemed to be progressive and full of good ideas, their managers did not all subscribe to the corporate communications plans, strategies, or administrative systems. These organizations were not led by top executives who created and sustained strong performance value cultures, and this was the major problem these companies faced. Replacing a key leader is not an easy task; however, having a good boss is essential to successful performance—employee and corporate.

Unfortunately, it sometimes is necessary to replace the key leader in order to modify the culture of a company. The company culture cannot be completely improved by management actions alone, the top leader must be working for the change, too. If the leader is not effectively establishing and communicating SPVs within the organization, it is unlikely that the culture can be changed and that the corporate financial performance can be improved. When culture is moved from one company to another, it must be transplanted at the level of the key leader. Whether this is accomplished by changes initiated by the present leader, by the hiring of a key leader from another company with an SPVC, or by the promotion of an executive who manages his or her portion of the mixed performance value culture by SPVs is unimportant; what is essential is that the cultural change be instigated and overseen by the person at the top of the company, who has a free hand to institute the change.

The obstruction of the leader's actions can be a problem in companies that have strong investor representatives who are overseeing the company from some position above the key leader. These people can inhibit the cultural change process, although, because they are not operational managers, they cannot institute an SPVC. What is essential is the presence of a leader who not only is qualified professionally to implant SPVs in the company but also has the authority to do so. Culture change requires that management authority be invested in the office of the key leader. He or she may elect to share management power; however, it must be in the office of the leader originally.

In most of the cases where a strong, performance-driven culture has not been transplanted successfully, the company identified a new key leader but left someone in the chairman position who espoused the old and less satisfactory culture. In such a situation, managers lower in the organization are not likely to believe that cultural change is necessary or desirable. A lot of time and energy may be expended trying to accomplish the cultural change, but if the person occupying the most powerful position does not back the effort the culture will remain mixed and the company will continue to perform poorly.

How to Change Company Culture

It does not make any difference what kind of administrative systems a company uses if the company does not have a culture that communicates and reinforces strong performance values. To be effective, the SPVs must be ingrained in the culture and reinforced by financial and nonfinancial rewards. The key leader must believe it is in the best interests of all parties to manage by SPVs. All the incentive plans and performance-appraisal systems in the world will not make up for a lack of high-level commitment to strong performance values. The culture determines how a company does; administrative systems cannot make up for a weak or mixed performance-value culture. They can, however, be used to help change to, communicate, and reinforce an SPVC.

All administrative systems can be hung on to a weak or mixed performance value culture as well as associated with a strong performance value culture. They are only helpers, although all too often they are used in place of a system of communications and rewards that reinforces constructive behavior.

The Leader's Role

When considering how to improve the company's performance, the key executive must first determine what kind of culture he or she is directing. If the company does not include SPVs as an essential management priority, the key leader must determine whether the culture can be changed to an SPVC. Too often, the leader will try to institute change at lower management levels, which will do little, except perhaps to change a weak performance value culture into a mixed performance value culture, assuming the leader is fortunate enough to find some managers who manage by SPVs.

Leaders of companies with weak or mixed performance value cultures may have the capacity to manage their companies with SPVs, but they do not know how to go about instituting the values. By learning how to establish SPVs and communicate them through administrative systems, they can change their corporate cultures and improve their firms' financial performance.

If a top executive realizes that he or she is the reason the company is doing poorly, but believes he or she can manage by SPVs, there is a good chance the company can change its culture. The most difficult (and sometimes unrealistic) part of this scenario is the leader's realization that he or she is the problem. It is a rare executive who can admit that. Companies themselves tend to look for, and find, someone other than the leader to blame for the lack of financial success, and many organizations have made major personnel changes, only to continue to perform at a less than excellent level because the key leader has not been replaced. Performance improvement begins with the key leader.

The Role of Strong Performance Values

In business today, productivity counts more than ever. The company that is most productive is the company that is most profitable. However, no productivity improvement plans can compensate for the absence of a culture that consistently reinforces for and communicates to all employees what forms of performance are important. Specific guidance about how to perform better is what can improve performance. This guidance must come from the foundation of the organization—its culture—and this is why SPVs are so important. SPVs, once established, make all the administrative systems of the organization work well.

Key leaders of SPV companies attribute the success of their companies to their cultures and their strong performance values. How and why these leaders evaluate alternatives and make decisions; develop and implement their sales, marketing, and other plans; and institute any administrative systems can be attributed to the company's strong performance values. No key leader in a successful high technology company is able to associate the success of the company with anything the company does other than its management by SPVs. The constant determiner of success is the existence of SPVs.

The strong performance values used to manage a company must be clear and precise. They cannot be mere slogans, no matter how high sounding. The best strong performance values are those that cause action or inspire innovation. The administrative systems must be associated with the SPVC. For example, when an SPV stipulates that the organization will increase the worth of the company to the shareholders by a specific amount over a particular period of time, an administrative system such as a management compensation program must be designed to respond directly to this SPV.

The slogan, "to improve corporate net worth," is not an SPV because it is too general: the company can do little to operationalize this objective. An SPV must define specifically how to improve the company's net worth. SPVs should never be copied from another company. This book does not include the specific SPVs of the successful companies for that reason. It is important that top executives spend time developing and implementing their own strong performance values so that the SPVs are truly part of the corporate culture.

The Managers' Role

Managers must subscribe to the key leader's strong performance values. They must use the SPVs in the management of their areas and make sure that administrative objectives that are intended to support the SPVC are well integrated and coordinated in their areas. The executives in the core group must communicate and reinforce the strong performance values of the key leader in their dealings with managers and other employees. Having a pool of strong managers who support the key leader's views and methods provides for cultural continuity in the company and avoids the problem of not having an adequate supply of executives with homogeneous strong performance values to sustain the high performance of the company.

Strong performance values, such as profit performance and technical excellence, can become outdated or diluted if they are established by a key executive who is not in contact with the operations of the company and the outside world. Consistent and intensive testing of the company's interpretation of the SPVs must take place. This is a management function, not the job of a market research or business planning group. The leader and the core group of operating executives must spend time with customers and understand competitors' products or services. Management by staff reports is not practiced by executives in the companies that perform the best; these executives do not leave the information gathering process to a staff organization. Little or nothing is lost in data interpretation because the executives themselves are finding out what changes must be made to the SPVs, to their communications channels, and to their application by evaluating how the SPVs are doing in the outside world and making any changes they feel are needed to keep the SPVs responsive to market and company needs.

The Role of the Compensation Program

Administrative systems are the best SPVC helpers. However, the administrative systems in companies with weak or mixed performance value cultures often are designed more to protect the company from the process of management than to help expedite the management process. These systems must be repaired if an SPVC is to be established and financial performance is to be driven by factors other than the consequences of general business conditions and the influence of external markets. In companies that perform well, the administrative systems communicate the strong performance values; they do not hinder the management process, they help it.

Management compensation programs are based on performance criteria that are important to the attainment of the SPVs. The design of a compensation program interprets the SPVs so that its administration will communicate the SPVs throughout the company. An observer should be able to find out what a company's SPVs are by reviewing the management compensation program. The reward systems for managers must be consistent with what the key leader of a company with an SPVC wants accomplished. Programs should be flexible and easily changed. They are part of the effective management process, and when they no longer make good business sense, they should be changed.

The basic compensation tools that help to reinforce and communicate SPVs were reviewed earlier in this book. As was stressed in that discussion, it is the tinkerer who gets the best results with the administrative systems. This individual takes standard programs and changes them to meet the needs of his or her company. When an administrative system fails to do the job, the tinkerer replaces or modifies it. In this way, an administrative system becomes a means to an end, sustaining high performance and productivity, rather than an end itself.

When tinkering, there is nothing wrong with trying management fads; some work very well. However, whatever fad is adopted, it must be associated with the strong performance values of the company. Management by objectives, sensitivity training, and other popular management techniques may work for individuals, but if the corporate culture does not support them, disillusionment will result from their use in a company. If a management fad is simply a way to measure financial performance in companies that are not doing well, it should not be used with the hope that it will get people to work together cooperatively. The role of management techniques and administrative systems must not be confused with the role of SPVs. The techniques and systems must be linked to the SPVC and they must communicate the SPVs, but techniques and systems will come and go. The performance-driven culture will survive (and try out other systems) as long as it is championed by top management.

Management decisions can be made more quickly and effectively when the basic foundation for reaching decisions is well established. The organization can only stick to basics if some basics exist. An organization's basics are, by definition, cultural; SPVs shape the culture that serves as the foundation for performance. Administrative systems must be designed to help that culture work. That is their role.

The Employees' Role

People are the key to success. An important strong performance value deals with the contribution of the individual to the overall success of the company. Companies that perform well treat people as important members of the culture who deserve respect and appropriate rewards as a result of working successfully in the company. Management by SPVs depends on communication with people. Everyone must know what the rules of the game are and how they as individuals fit into the corporate picture.

The companies with SPVCs have as their employees people who are excited about what they are doing. These employees view themselves as productive and are confident about the roles they play in their companies' plans. They are not pampered, they are just turned on to their importance to the company and the other people with whom they work. Clear communications that tell people what they are supposed to be doing is an accurate and consistent way help to motivate employees. Being rewarded for behavior that is consistent with the SPVs also motivates people.

Questioning the Way Things Are

The successful companies constantly question the way they are doing things. Asking questions about how the SPVs are being reinforced and communicated is appropriate organizationally. Questioning is part of a manager's job. Employees should be encouraged to constructively seek reasons for why things are being done one way and not another. Asking questions can only serve to improve performance and clarify objectives.

Encouraging employees to ask questions requires that managers talk to people rather than use administrative systems as barriers to face-to-face contact. Because managers must ask questions in order to implement and interpret the strong performance values, they should expect their people to ask questions, too. Questioning provides the company with the opportunity to evaluate alternative ways of doing things. A good question can lead to an answer nobody thought of before, to a way of accomplishing something with less expense or faster. Asking good questions of top management, then, is important to good performance and should be part of a company's improved culture.

Improving Compensation Programs

Historically, management compensation programs have been designed for companies in basic industries, not for high technology companies. The programs some high technology companies have adopted are more appropriate for firms that have a stable growth rate or that dominate a particular market. The leaders of companies that perform well prefer custom-designed reward systems that recognize the dynamics of the high technology industry and that reward team work. Key executives are emphasizing new management compensation priorities, including the following:

1. Short-term incentive plans that can be installed and used in a more flexible way to reward the performance of managers and communicate to them that working cooperatively is worthwhile. Group, rather than individual, performance must be communicated, reinforced, and rewarded.

2. Long-term incentive plans that are relevant to the importance of the tasks assigned to managers. Priority is given to plans that offer managers an equity position in the company in exchange for sustained good performance that supports strong performance values.
3. Job evaluation systems that measure the actual responsibilities of management jobs. A system that associates job worth with group performance standards and that communicates the specific job skills each manager must perform to be in step with the company's performance values is desired.

In the successful companies, tinkerers are already at work modifying the basic management compensation programs to meet their companies' specific needs. Some of the changes compensation program tinkerers in the companies with strong performance value cultures are making focus on the following areas:

1. Criteria selection: More effort is being expended to select better long- and short-term qualitative and quantitative performance criteria. These criteria are oriented toward rewarding managers who work well as a team. The rewarding of individual performance is restricted to jobs below the management level, if it is done at all.
2. New equity devices: New ways of sharing company ownership are being explored. How to use stock, stock options, and other programs more creatively is being considered in order to meet the need to share more of the success with the managers responsible for it.
3. Equal opportunities: Because many more women are entering management in high technology companies, improved methods of determining the actual worth of the jobs are being sought to counteract the discrimination that many feel exists in current high technology management teams.

The push for more team-oriented compensation plans comes from the dissatisfaction high technology companies feel toward their current plans. A lot of improvements made to compensation plans will come from these companies' inventing new administrative systems of adapting old ones to match their cultures. The companies with strong performance value cultures are far ahead of others in the redesigning of management compensation programs.

Trends in Total Management Compensation

Companies need to evaluate and compare the components of total compensation programs, including not only base salaries and cash incentives, but also long-term incentives such as stock plans, direct stock awards, stock options, and restricted stock options. Also, measuring the financial worth of plans such as performance share/unit, phantom stock and sequential award plans that pay out either cash or stock, and management perquisites and special benefits is required. Once gathered, this information serves as the starting point for compensation planning. A company with a specific philosophy will want its total compensation program to reflect that philosophy and, therefore, will want to know which plans will do that best.

Compensation objectives identify the role rewards play in the management of the company. The objectives must link the financial and non-financial rewards to the corporate SPVs. Objectives also should be used to periodically evaluate existing compensation plans to make sure they are continuing to respond to the performance values of the company. Compensation plans must not become stagnant. The industry is moving too fast for a company to rely on an inflexible administrative system.

By continually evaluating compensation plans in terms of how well they fit the organization's needs, the key leader is seeking better ways of rewarding managers. The competition is not going to relax its efforts, and neither should any smart top executive. Looking for the one best way to reward good managers, even though it may not be attainable, and tinkering with the management compensation process to see how closely it can be aligned with strong performance values is what good management compensation practice is all about.

Much of what has been discussed so far has focused on designing effective administrative systems that help an organization attain its objectives. It is important to remember that administrative systems are value free; that is, they obtain their values elsewhere—ideally, from the strong performance values of the company. The systems must be adapted to meet changing situations so that they help the company communicate and reinforce its performance values. All administrative systems, including the management-compensation program, must be well integrated. As has been stressed throughout this book, systems must effectively interpret and communicate what the organization is attempting to accomplish.

How the Best Performers Plan Compensation

The companies that perform the best use their administrative systems to communicate their strong performance values and, therefore, follow a similar approach to compensation program development. Keeping in mind that the central purpose of the program is to communicate a message to managers and the entire employee population, key leaders must approach the development of management compensation programs from the standpoint of their usability as communication tools. The message the programs carry is of singular importance to the programs' design.

Compensation Objectives. The best performers develop management-compensation objectives that are more than slogans and use them as evaluative criteria to guide the compensation program development process. Compensation objectives outline the relationship between each element of management compensation and the SPVs of the company. For example, rather than merely suggest that the purpose of a job evaluation plan is to create internal equity between management jobs and to develop a competitive management pay structure, the objectives state, in detail, the compensable factors that will be used to determine the worth of management jobs in terms of their contribution to the attainment of SPVs. One factor will evaluate the impact jobs have on the financial performance of the company; another factor will reflect the worth of jobs in the area of human resource management.

In some cases, the development of objectives is an integral part of the general business planning process. In other cases, they may be developed separately. When they are developed separately, they are nonetheless tied to the rest of the business plans of the company in order to ensure that the reward systems are consistent with what the company is trying to do overall.

Evaluation of Alternatives. A key leader uses the compensation objectives, and the corresponding SPVs, to determine the best mix of compensation programs for the company. Few leaders believe that management compensation programs can remain constant for long periods of time and still respond to the changing needs of business. Certain approaches to management compensation may be useful for a period of time, but they are bound to be replaced by other programs as the business variables and needs of the company change. Thus, the key leaders of companies that perform well frequently reevaluate the effectiveness of their compensation programs. Their evaluations are based on how well the programs assist them and their executives in communicating strong performance values. They also look at the practices of other companies to determine any possible advantage that might be gained by adopting competitors' programs. Any plan that evaluates the performance of the management group rather than the individual is considered. A little me-too compensation planning goes on in the best of firms. However, if a competitor's plan is adopted, it probably will be adapted, too, to fit the company's specific needs.

The management compensation programs should be reviewed on a continuing basis. Because the systems are designed as tools of communication, and communications needs change, the programs in the best companies are developed to permit modification of the way they communicate SPVs.

Job Evaluation Solutions. The leaders in the successful companies prefer to use the point-factor approach to job evaluation because they believe a quantitative approach is better suited to companies that emphasize engineering management. Also, the point-factor plan allows them to develop compensable factors that reflect their SPVs and show managers what components are most important in their jobs.

Some executives are interested in using a totally qualitative program, such as the knowledge and abilities approach described earlier. It is likely there will be more experimentation with this type of program in the future. However, at the present time, most key leaders are focusing on custom designing an approach to job evaluation that includes some version of the point-factor methodology.

Salary Administration Solutions. The companies that perform well pay base salaries that are higher than the average salaries their labor market competitors pay for similar jobs. The twenty-four top performers in the study paid an average base salary for management jobs that was 5 percent or more above the average base salary paid for similar jobs by the companies that perform less successfully.

The leaders of the good performers say that their base salary levels are higher than those of other companies because, although the larger salaries represent an additional expense, the salaries provide peace of mind to members of the management group. Also, the key leaders believe that managers are the important communicators of the SPVs and expending a little more money is justifiable if it helps to retain a constant cadre of managers who manage by SPVs.

In addition to paying higher base salaries to their managers, the better corporate performers also tend to grant base salary increases more frequently than once a year, which is the industry practice for management-level personnel. Pay progression is over 5 percent faster for managers in the SPV companies than it is for managers in other companies. The faster pay progression is intended to indicate to managers their importance to the continued successful performance of the company. Key leaders of these companies say that more frequent pay increases encourages management teamwork and the communication of SPVs.

The key leaders of good performers are not big fans of using base-salary increases to try to recognize individual performance. Most are searching for a credible way to distribute pay increases on the basis of group performance. However, until they find such an approach, they are not strongly committed to granting base salary increases in recognition of individual performance. Instead, they tend to reserve the recognition of performance differences for their incentive plans. Because variable compensation is not built into a manager's base salary permanently, the compensation can be awarded to different individuals or groups each year. The key leaders view the granting of awards through incentive plans as more meaningful than the granting of pay increases through the salary administration process because the rewards can be linked more closely to specific achievements and objectives.

Incentive Plan Solutions. Organizations that succeed financially emphasize flexible incentive plans because their leaders believe good performance is best attained if the incentive plans can be designed to reward group performance and include many qualitative criteria that communicate the incremental steps that must be taken to attain the companies' SPVs. Including qualitative criteria in their short-term incentive plans enables executives to manage and reward a wider range of performance. The qualitative criteria show how a group of managers, brought together to solve common problems and meet similar challenges, must work collectively. Financial criteria can set objectives, but they cannot communicate methodology.

The incentive plans the companies with strong performance value cultures use include stock options, incentive stock options, and junior stock options as well as direct stock awards. In addition, many use restricted stock plans with both qualitative and quantitative restrictions attached to the plans. As a result of the use of these plans, members of the top three or four levels of management in these companies have the opportunity to attain ownership positions.

The best performers also use a number of nonstock plans to emphasize performance that is not directly measurable through the price of company stock. These plans award capital at the end of their performance periods. The awards are substantially greater than those made for management participation in long-term plans in the companies that perform less well.

Perquisites and Benefit Solutions. There is little difference between the extra benefits and perquisites offered to managers in the most successful companies and those offered in the less successful ones, although the use of variable benefits is gaining popularity among good performers. The less satisfactory performers seem to offer more liberal and expensive management benefits than do the better performers. Good corporate performance and elaborate management benefits do not seem to go together. The key leaders of the successful companies spend money on incentives and salaries rather than on extra indirect compensation for management personnel. The best performers also tend to offer more liberal general employee benefits which may be why they offer fewer extra management benefits and perquisites.

Communication of Performance Values

Because the management compensation programs in the more profitable companies are designed to communicate the companies' performance values, their distribution of rewards tends to be less automatic. Their administration requires additional time because the programs integrate the processes of managing and rewarding. Their use of a combination of financial criteria and qualitative criteria and their emphasis on team work rather than individual accomplishments help top management communicate strong performance values and also require the managers to work cooperatively in order to succeed within their firms.

Tinkering adapts standard approaches to management compensation planning to the specific needs of a company. The follow-up part of tinkering is the continuing evaluation of the programs once they are in place. To evaluate the appropriateness of a compensation program, the key leader determines whether the program is continuing to communicate the message he or she wants reinforced throughout the company. In the companies that perform poorly, the management process and the compensation programs are not linked. Instead, the administrative systems tend to replace the face-to-face process of management. Perhaps this is why these companies' financial rewards to their managers lack the communications impact that most incentive plans are intended to have.

Summary: High Technology Innovation

High technology companies are in the process of establishing themselves. They are, as a result, more open to experimenting with different approaches to management and are less apt to be dedicated to specific administrative methods. Their willingness to try new or different approaches, to be innovative, may benefit companies in other industries. The same principles apply to any company that is willing to evaluate and improve its culture. The principles of business are similar, regardless of the company's product or service. As long as the key leader believes the employees are the company's principal asset and is willing to establish and reinforce a culture that communicates the importance of performance, that leader has a good opportunity to improve the financial performance of the company.

The only advantage high technology companies have over other companies is their experience with the creative use of administrative systems. The western business world is well acquainted with administrative systems. What other companies need to learn is how to integrate their administrative systems into their cultures—and perhaps how to shape their cultures so that they communicate strong performance values. If a change in culture is required, then the administrative systems will have to be modified subsequently in order to assist in the communications of the newly established strong performance values.

Changing the form of administrative systems to assist the culture in the reinforcement and communications of SPVs is not easy, but it is much less difficult than changing culture. However, culture can be changed, given the right circumstances, and administrative systems can be used to strengthen culture. When corporate culture is already consistent with strong performance values but the administrative systems do not support the cultures, changing the systems so they assist the management process just makes sense.

Much research concerning how to motivate people as individuals has been conducted. The information presented in this book suggests that it is more important to emphasize group performance that is consistent with what the key leader is trying to accomplish. More research on and theories about the motivation of groups and the importance of the culture to improved productivity is needed, but it seems clear that motivating the individual is not enough; the appropriate culture, which motivates people to work together, is what a company needs in order to succeed.

8

Epilog about
Better Performance

During the period of this book's research on culture and performance, a number of the sample companies with weak and mixed performance value cultures considered changing their cultures. They found the study's evidence of the idea that managing by strong performance values resulted in greatly improved financial performance convincing. At the time of this writing, the longest one of these companies has been involved in the change is a little over two years. Measuring any change takes at least eighteen months, so the results are not all in by any means. However, discussing a few of the companies that are in the process of cultural change will add to the information already presented about the use of management compensation programs. Also, it will provide the reader with the opportunity to learn about the process of change.

To show that company performance can be changed, three case histories of companies from the original study will be presented in this chapter. None of these companies was a bad performer; all were doing less well than they could, and their change to an SPVC seems to be improving their performance.

Case 1—XYZ Medical Technology, Inc.

Background

XYZ Medical is twelve years old. It develops, manufactures, and sells sophisticated electronic devices to the health-care industry. The company was venture capitalized and was directed for many years by two entrepreneurial scientists. With one or two market-dominating products, the company's sales and profits soared for the first eight years. Management style was paternalistic, and many employees earned significant direct stock awards and stock options. Salary and incentives were managed on an extremely personal basis. As the company grew, good scientists and engineers were made managers, but little time was spent on the management process. Staff organizations (marketing, personnel, advertising, and finance) grew and established whatever administrative systems were needed with only minimal intervention from operating management.

During the last several years, the high technology medical products field has attracted a large number of companies. As a result, competition for market share and the development of new technology has increased in this area. The profits, sales, and new technological developments of XYZ Medical fell off, although the company still performed at a satisfactory profit level for the industry. The key leaders had a strong culture based on honesty, fairness, good employee relations, employee participation in decision making, and leadership, but none of these values could be identified as a strong performance value. When profit performance leveled off, the company leadership was confused. It discovered that the company was managed by staff personnel, who were almost equal to the line personnel in number and exceeded them in authority.

Change in Process

The two founders and key leaders retired from the company after hiring a new chief executive and helping that new leader's transition into the company. The new key leader has developed strong performance values by modifying those used in his former place of employment to match XYZ Medical's needs. The new key leader is now developing a cadre of operating managers to help communicate and reinforce the strong performance value culture. Managers who were judged as capable of reinforcing and communicating the SPVs have been retained. Other managers have been either replaced or transferred to nonmanagement technical jobs. The responsibility for developing administrative systems has been retained by the new key leader and much of the supporting staff personnel have been eliminated. Short- and long-term incentives that use SPVs as performance criteria and a basic job-evaluation plan that determines the worth of a job based on its opportunity to have an impact on the SPVC are being developed. An intensive communications effort is now underway. The initial disruptive period is over, and employees are beginning to work better as a team.

Some new products are being developed to help the company regain a strong competitive position. The financial performance slide has lessened, with the help of some new capital acquired to restart the company. Cost reduction has resulted in a small profit increase this fiscal year. The key leader is active in the business and in the establishment of the SPVC. People are beginning to talk about SPVs, partly as a result of the first incentive awards having been granted to those whose performance was consistent with the strong performance values of the company. Nobody is talking about the good old days. Only the present and the future are being discussed.

Commentary

The motivation for the founders to step down was their large investment in the company and pressure from the board of directors. They did not recruit a new key leader in their own image but selected one from a successful organization whose culture is driven by strong performance values. The most important step in the process was replacing the founders and giving support to the new key leader. The establishment, communication, and reinforcement of the SPVs could not have been started without the leadership change.

Case 2—MNO Electronic Devices Corporation

Background

MNO is a spin-off of a large electronics company, and it was founded by a scientist who managed a large technology group for the larger company. MNO is ten years old. It grew rapidly due to the market success of a single sophisticated electronics product having broad military applications. Management style was unilateral, with the founder making nearly all decisions. The company went public several years ago to obtain capital. The incentive program included stock options and an annual plan that granted awards in a semiautomatic manner as a percent of base salary and on the basis of whether certain annual pretax profit objectives were attained.

Two years ago, the military began to phase out the vehicle that used MNO's electronic device, which caused a plateau in sales and profits at first. The founder added many new members to the technical staff and hired some professional managers to help the company diversify. These actions resulted in uneven teamwork and an inconsistent corporate culture (a mixed performance value culture). Company performance continued to flounder and profits fell off slightly, with no improvement in sight.

Change in Process

Two of the managers the key leader had obtained came from companies with strong performance value cultures, although the companies' primary SPVs differed. The leader formed an SPV task force with these managers to establish strong performance values for MNO and to develop a plan for communications and financial reinforcement. In this way, he hoped to retain the chief executive position and learn SPVs from the two operational managers.

The company has been reorganized under the two principal subordinates, and responsibility for communications and reinforcement of SPVs has been centralized with the expectation that, as more and more managers learn to manage by SPVs, the company will be decentralized gradually. Attainable SPVs with reasonable profit goals have been established and are being communicated. Heavy emphasis is placed on market analysis by executives and new product development by line personnel. The long- and short-term incentive plans use both qualitative and quantitative SPVs as performance criteria.

A new, nonmilitary electronic product has been developed for commercial application, and a sales force has been established. The key leader is spending a great deal of time in the organization communicating the SPVs of the company; people are talking about and questioning the SPVs. Employee attitudes are positive, and the company expects to make a measurable profit improvement during the current fiscal year. In general, the company is becoming more unified and cooperation is its byword.

Commentary

MNO's key leader was able to use managers from other companies with SPVCs to help manage by SPVs. This required a willingness to learn from subordinates that many top executives do not have. The leader is now in the process of establishing a culture based on strong performance values and, because of this, corporate performance seems to be improving and the company is in a better position to sustain future profitable performance. The key leader of MNO has helped to change the company culture in a positive manner.

Case 3—ABC Computer Technology, Inc.

Background

ABC Computer is sixteen years old. It develops and manufactures microcomputers and related hardware and software. As an early entrant into the field, the company carved a position for itself that permitted rapid and profitable growth for a number of years. A venture into electronic games proved unsuccessful, and the company returned to the business they knew best—small computers. However, competition increased and the company's investments in technological areas failed to provide them with a new product that was competitive from both a pricing and a technological standpoint.

The company has had several chief executives since its founding, and none of the original principles of the company are reflected in its current management. The company changed administrative systems (compensation programs, financial planning procedures, sales strategy, and so forth) with each new executive. Sales and profits leveled off after a new chief executive was hired a few years ago, but the board of directors has been hesitant to change top management again.

Change in Process

The financial performance of ABC Computer had been satisfactory but it was no longer excellent. To regain great performance, the board of directors and the chief executive developed some general strong performance values. The chief executive subsequently designed them to be specific to the company and formulated a strategy to establish a culture based upon these values. The key leader and his management team are now spending considerable effort carrying out an intensive, face-to-face communications plan that includes a reward system based on the strong performance values.

Because the leader had no experience in managing a performance-driven company, the change in culture has been a painful and time-consuming process. The first year was spent getting things going. By the end of the second year, after a sales compensation program consistent with the SPVs had been designed, computer sales began to improve. In addition, several strong and promising product lines are well under way. The company profit picture is improving, and ABC Computer is on its way to being an excellent performer once again.

Commentary

The ABC Computer company was performing at an acceptable level, but its board of directors wanted it to have excellent profit performance. The board decided that management continuity was important and vested the chief executive with the responsibility of developing SPVs and establishing an SPVC. Although lack of experience with managing by SPVs slowed the process, it was nonetheless possible for ABC Computer to improve its performance without changing its key leader.

Culture and Performance

The investigation for this book provided significant evidence to suggest that an appropriately developed company culture, one based on strong performance values, is an essential contributor to financial performance. Also, the research indicated that effectively designed management compensation programs are instrumental in the communication and reinforcement of the strong performance values. This suggests that the foundation for a management-compensation program should be the performance values of the corporate culture.

The cultural changes that have been observed since the research was conducted indicate that a key leader can modify the culture of the company and improve its financial performance. The company that is not performing up to financial expectations should expend management compensation dollars on the communication of SPVs.

A communications model for a company with a strong performance-value culture is shown in figure 8-1. Culture is at the foundation of the model and so serves as the base for reward systems. On the next level is the performance group, which is important to the cohesiveness of the company. Thus, reward systems communicate to the performance group (division or work unit) that achievement of the SPVs will be rewarded financially. On the top level is the individual, whose performance is important to the success of the performance group. The SPVs, then, are communicated to the individual through the performance group, which learns of the SPVs by way of the reward system. The individual learns, therefore, how important his or her performance is to making the performance group successful and, in turn, how important group performance is to company success.

In a company with an SPVC, the emphasis is placed on designing systems that are communication tools rather than mechanisms that in some way attempt to manipulate or cajole the individual to behave in some manner. The individual benefits because he or she gets a piece of the action as a result of contributing to the group. The performance group benefits by receiving more clearly defined messages about how performance is to be achieved and how it will be rewarded. The company benefits because it has a much better chance of attaining the performance it wants. This structure reflects the importance of culture on the behavior of small groups and the motives of the individual.

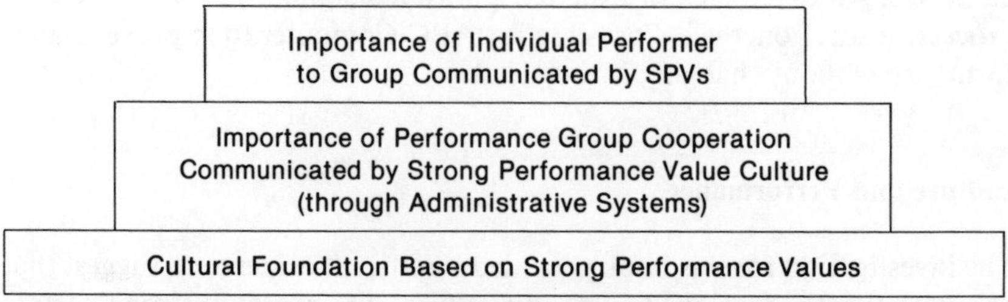

Figure 8-1. The Culture/Performance Schematic

Summary

What the research for this book and the in-process changes described in this chapter show is the power of well-designed administrative systems that reflect the values of an SPVC. Most important, the results of the investigation show that an SPVC integrates the financial objectives and the human resources objectives of the company. The practitioner who worries about the behavioral implications of compensation programs must also be concerned about the financial aspects of these plans. Additionally, the financier cannot expect a company to perform merely because it has an awards system. The plan also must provide for the company's human resources by considering the implications of culture, small group behaviors, and individuals' differences. All these things were known but companies needed a practical application of the theories in order to improve their financial performance.

Additional effort should be expended in showing companies how to develop and operationalize strong performance values. Because western corporations already know a great deal about administrative systems, it makes sense for them to use this knowledge to make their companies perform in a more satisfactory manner. The systems are the best way to communicate SPVs throughout an organization. With the coordinated efforts of key leaders, managers, planners in the areas of compensation and human resource management, and financial analysts, corporate cultures can be improved and companies can be successful performers.

Appendix:
The Research
Background

All of the book's conclusions concerning the roles culture and management-compensation programs play in company performance are based on extensive interviews and analysis of written material in a sample of high technology companies. The thrust of the investigation was the exploration of the relationship between organizational performance-related values and management reward systems in growing high technology companies. It was not reasonable to write about the performance of high technology companies without a fresh review of these organizations because they are too dynamic.

In order to develop a sound empirical foundation for the investigation, a sample of one hundred financially successful high technology companies having sales of from $156 to $680 million was selected. The organizations selected showed, over the last five years, average increases in sales that substantially exceeded the average increases of the industry in general. The sales figures have been adjusted for inflation. During the same period, the companies also had net profit increases that were much greater than those in the high technology industry in general. In 1982, the target sample averaged annual sales of $492 million and had median sales of $412 million. Sixty-six of the organizations provided complete information. The sales of this group averaged $504 million, with a median of $496 million. These sixty-six organizations accurately represent the one hundred companies originally selected for research. Among a group of companies that performed well, some were exceptional performers. These were the SPVC companies.

Survey Methodology

The best way to determine what key leaders and decision makers think about management compensation is to talk to them face to face. The investigators met personally with everyone who agreed to provide enough time to answer the necessary questions. Therefore, in each of the sixty-six companies, investigators either spoke directly to the chairman, chief executive officer, chief operating officer, or whatever person was identified as the company's key leader.

All the investigators had experience in management interviewing. The same interviewers were used for all information gathering. Each investigator was coached on the information desired. The investigation team role-played many executive interviews before the visits were scheduled, and a patterned investigation format was utilized in each instance to make sure everyone obtained information in a similar manner. As a result, the executives spoke to the interviewers in a very open and sharing way, and the interchanges were reported to be useful both to the executives and to the investigators.

Differences between the Participants

The key leaders varied in their perceptions of their industry, of what makes a company successful, and of the role management compensation plays in the direction of organizations. The cultures of the companies also varied. Some companies had basic performance values that were perceived in the same way by the key leaders, their lieutenants, and lower managers. These organizations had a more socialized view about their objectives and what their management team should be trying to accomplish. In other organizations, managers had more divergent views of what their companies were attempting to do. These organizations tended to have more heterogeneous performance values.

In some companies, management compensation plans were important aids to the communication of the objectives of the organization. In the companies where key leaders played an important role in compensation plan design, but not necessarily its day-to-day administration, management compensation was likely to be viewed as a management priority. In the companies where management compensation was considered less important to the direction of company operations, top managers described their compensation programs almost wholly in terms of the competitive realities of the high technology market place rather than as a valuable ingredient to corporate success. Differences also existed in the companies' approaches to job evaluation, short-term and long-term incentives, as well as management perquisites. Some of the differences that existed between the companies are significant, considering the industry is fairly homogeneous from a professional standpoint.

High technology organizations compete with each other not only for market share but also for technical and managerial talent and the development of technology. The organizations grow out of each other; that is, bright technologists often leave one company to start another, transplanting culture, values, and administrative practices. The large and successful high technology companies influence their off-shoot companies. Either the new company attempts to adopt a similar culture because the key leader likes the organization from which he or she came, or it may adopt a culture that is the antithesis of the culture the key leader left if he or she did not like the former employer.

Implications of the Research

The research indicated that organizations with the key leaders who communicate strong performance values and establish a strong performance-value culture direct the most profitable companies. Although the remaining companies performed acceptably well, only the SPVC companies were top financial performers. It suggested that the companies that do not manage with the use of SPVs do less well financially.

Although the investigators looked for other factors that would have a predictable impact on performance, the research showed no other organizational or cultural variables that accounted for the difference in the companies' financial performance. The study indicated that culture would be changed by the key leader's introducing SPVs and that the cultural changes would result in improved financial performance. This information gives some hope to the less successful organizations that are earnestly seeking a way to improve their performance.

Bibliography

Argyris, Chris. "Today's Problems with Tomorrow's Organizations." *Journal of Management Studies* (February 1967):31–55.

Atchison, Thomas, and Wendell French. "Pay Systems for Scientists and Engineers." *Industrial Relations* 7, no. 1 (October 1967):44–56.

Barnard, Chester I. *The Functions of the Executive.* Cambridge, Mass.: Harvard University Press, 1938.

Barnard, Chester I., *Organization and Management.* Cambridge, Mass: Harvard University Press, 1962.

Behrend, Hilde. "Financial Incentives as the Expression of a System of Beliefs." *British Journal of Sociology* 10, no. 2 (June 1959).

Belcher, D.W. "The Changing Nature of Compensation Administration." *California Management Review* (Summer 1969):89–94.

Belcher, David W. *Compensation Administration.* Englewood Cliffs, N.J.: Prentice-Hall, 1974.

Bell, Daniel. *In the Computer Age: A Twenty Year Retrospective.* Edited by Michael L. Dertouzos and Joel Moses. Cambridge, Mass.: M.I.T. Press, 1969.

Blumrosen, Ruth G. "Wage Discrimination, Job Segregation, and Title VII of the Civil Rights Act of 1964." *Michigan Journal of Law Reform* (Spring 1979).

Bower, Marvin. *The Will to Manage.* New York: McGraw-Hill, 1966.

Brinks, James T. "Executive Compensation: Crossroads of the '80's." *Personnel Administrator* (December 1981):23–28.

Briscoe, Dennis R. "Organizational Design: Dealing with the Human Constraint." *California Management Review* (Fall 1980):71–80.

Bronstein, Richard J. "The Equity Component of the Executive Compensation Package." *California Management Review* (Fall 1980):64–70.

Bronstein, Richard J. "Making Incentives Rational for Executives and Stockholders." *Personnel Journal* 54, no. 1 (January 1975):22–24, 63.

Brumback, Gary B. "Consolidating Job Descriptions, Performance Appraisals, and Manpower Reports." *Personnel Journal* 50, no. 8 (August 1971):604–610.

Carroll, Stephen J., Jr., and Henry L. Tosi, Jr. *Management by Objectives: Applications and Research.* New York: Macmillan Co., 1973.

Carey, James F. "Successors to the Qualified Stock Option." *Harvard Business Review* (January-February 1978):140–146.

Cash, William H. "Executive Compensation." *Personnel Administrator* (September 1977):22–24, 35–36.

Cheeks, James E., and Gordon D. Wolf. *How to Compensate Executives.* Homewood, Ill.: Dow Jones—Irwin, 1979.

Cohn, Theodore, and Roy A. Lindberg. *Compensating Key Executives in the Smaller Company.* New York: AMACOM, 1979.

Cook, Fred. "The Changing Goals of Compensation." *Business Management* (February 1970):23–24.

Cook, Frederick W. "The Revenue Act of 1978 and Employee Compensation." *Compensation Review* (First Quarter 1979):22–30.

County of Washington v. *Gunther.* 452 U.S. 68 L. Ed. 2d 751, 25 FEP Cases 1521 No. 80–429, decided June 8, 1981.

Crystal, Graef S., and James W. Walker. "Executive Compensation: The Organizational Interface." *Compensation Review* (Fourth Quarter 1973):24–29.

Crystal, Graef S. *Executive Compensation.* New York: AMACOM, 1970.

Crystal, Graef S. "Motivating for the Future: The Long-Term Incentive Plan." *Financial Executive* (October 1971):48–50.

Crystal, Graef S. "The Ten Commandments of Executive Compensation." *Financial Executive* (August 1970):52–54.

Crystal, Graef, S. "This Time Stock Options Are Dead." *Business Management* (February 1970):42–43.

Cummings, Larry L., and Donald P. Schwab. *Performance in Organizations: Determinants and Appraisal.* Glenview, Ill.: Scott, Foresman and Co., 1973.

Day, Charles R., and Perry Pascarella. "Righting the Productivity Balance." *Industry Week* (September 29, 1980):44–47, 50.

Deal, Terrence E., and Allan A. Kennedy. *Corporate Cultures.* Menlo Park, Calif.: Addison-Wesley, 1982.

Devanna, Mary Anne; Charles Fombrun; and Noel Tichy. "Human Resource Management: A Strategic Perspective." *Organizational Dynamics* (Winter 1981):51–67.

Drucker, Peter F. *Concept of Corporation.* New York: John Jay, 1972.

Drucker, Peter F. *Management: Tasks, Responsibilities, Practices.* New York: Harper and Row, 1974.

Ellig, Bruce R. "Compensation Management: Its Past and Its Future." *Personnel* 54, no. 3 (1977):30–40.

Ellis, R. Jeffrey. "Improving Managment Response in Turbulent Times." *Sloan Management Review* (Winter 1982):3–12.

Fasching, Darrell J. "A Case for Corporate and Management Ethics." *California Management Review* (Summer 1981):62–76.

Flowers, Vincent S., and Charles L. Hughes. "Why Employees Stay." *Harvard Business Review* (July-August 1973):49–60.

Foster, Kenneth E., and Jill Kanin-Lovers. "Determinants of Organizational Pay Policies" *Compensation Review* 9, no. 3 (1977):35–41.

Foster, Kenneth E. "Accounting for Management Pay Differentials." *Industrial Relations* (October 1969):80–87.

Fruhan, W.E., Jr. *The Fight for Competitive Advantage.* Cambridge, Mass.: Division of Research, Harvard Graduate School of Business Administration, 1972.

Galbraith, Jay. *Organization Design.* Reading, Mass.: Addison-Wesley, 1977.

Goodman, Stanley J. *How to Manage a Turnaround.* New York: The Free Press, 1982.

Ginzberg, Eli, and Ewing Reilley. *Effecting Change in Large Organizations.* New York: Columbia University Press, 1959.

Greiner, Larry E. "Evolution and Revolution as Organizations Grow." *Harvard Business Review* (July-August 1972):37–46.

Hampton, David R., et al. *Organizational Behavior and The Practice of Management.* Glenview, Ill.: Scott, Foresman and Co., 1968.

Hardy, Charles. *Understanding Organizations.* New York: Penguin Books, 1976.

Hayes, Robert H., and William J. Abernathy. "Managing Our Way to Economic Decline." *Harvard Business Review* (July-August 1980):67–77.

Herzberg, Frederick. "One More Time: How Do You Motivate Employees?" *Harvard Business Review* (January-February 1968):53–62.

Hinrichs, John R. *The Motivation Crisis.* New York: AMACOM, 1974.

Humble, John W. *How to Manage by Objectives.* New York: American Management Associations, 1973.

Idema, Thomas H. "Systems Career Path Development." *Journal of Systems Management* 29, no. 4 (April 1978):30–35.

IUE v. *Westinghouse Electric* 631 F.2d 1984, 23 FEP Cases 588, 3d Cir. 1980. Cert. denied, 449 U.S. 1009, 1981.

Judson, Horace F. *Search for Solutions.* New York: Holt, Rinehart, and Winston, 1980.

Ketchum, Bradford W., Jr. "How Much Do the Top Execs Make?" *INC.* (July 1980):34–42.

Kiechel, Walter. "The Real World Strikes Back." *Fortune* (December 27, 1982):34–39.

Klein, Michael F., Jr. "Executive Perquisites." *Financial Executive* (March 1979):16–24.

Kuhn, Thomas S. *The Structure of Scientific Revolutions.* 2d. ed. Chicago, Ill.: University of Chicago Press, 1970.

Kutscher, Ronald E.; Jerome A. Mark; and John R. Norsworthy. "The Productivity Slowdown and the Outlook to 1985." *Monthly Labor Review* 200, no. 5 (May 1977):3– .

Lawler, Edward E., III. *Pay and Organizational Effectiveness: A Psychological View.* New York: McGraw-Hill, 1971.

Lemons v. *City and County of Denver.* 620 F.2d 228, 22 FEP Cases 959, 10th Cir. 1980. Cert. denied, 449 U.S. 888, 1980.

Levinson, Harry. *The Exceptional Executive.* Cambridge, Mass.: Harvard University Press, 1968.

Lohr, Steve. "Overhauling America's Business Management. *New York Times Magazine,* January 4, 1981.

March, James, and H. Simon. *Organizations.* New York: Wiley, 1958.

Maslow, Abraham H. *The Farther Reaches of Human Nature.* New York: Viking, 1971.

McGregor, Douglas. *The Human Side of Enterprise.* New York: McGraw-Hill, 1960.

McLaughlin, David J. "Reinforcing Corporate Strategy through Executive Compensation." *Management Review* (October 1981):8–15.

Nadler, David A., and E.E. Lawler, III "Motivation: A Diagnostic Approach." In *Perspectives on Behavior in Organizations,* edited by J.R. Hackman, E.E. Lawler, and L. Porter. New York: McGraw-Hill 1977.

Nash, Allan N., and Stephen J. Carroll, Jr. *The Management of Compensation.* Monterey, Calif.: Brooks Cole, 1975.

Nielsen, Richard P. "Toward a Method for Building Consensus During Strategic Planning." *Sloan Management Review* (Summer 1981):29–40.

Otis, Jay L., and Richard H. Leukart. *Job Evaluation.* 2d. ed. New York: Prentice-Hall, 1954.

Ohmae, Kenichi. *The Mind of the Strategist.* New York: McGraw-Hill, 1982.

Ouchi, William G. *Theory Z.* Menlo Park, Calif.: Addison-Wesley, 1981.

Pascale, Richard T., and Anthony G. Athos. *The Art of Japanese Management.* New York: Simon and Schuster, 1981.

Pearce, John A. "The Company Mission as a Strategic Tool." *Sloan Management Review* (Spring 1982):15–24.

Peters, Thomas J., and Robert H. Waterman, Jr. *In Search of Excellence.* New York: Harper and Row, 1982.

Peters, Thomas J. "Doing The Little Things Well." *Efficiencies, Effectiveness, Productivity.* September 1980.

Peters, Thomas J. "Leadership: Sad Facts and Silver Linings." *Harvard Business Review* 57, no. 6 (November-December 1979):164–172.

Peters, Thomas J. "Management Systems: The Language of Organizational Character and Competence." *Organizational Dynamics* (Summer 1980):2–26.

Peters, Thomas J. "Putting Excellence into Management." *Business Week* (July 21, 1980):196–205.

Porter, Michael E. *Competitive Strategy.* New York: The Free Press, 1980.

Praz, Richard P. "Compensation's Fickle Future." *The Personnel Administrator* (May-June 1972):29– .

Rappaport, Alfred. "Executive Incentives vs. Corporate Growth." *Harvard Business Review* (July-August 1978):81–88.

Rhodes, Lucien, and Cathryn Jakobson. "Small Companies: America's Hope for the 80s." *INC.* (April 1981):34–44.

Rogers, Carl. *On Becoming a Person.* New York: Houghton Mifflin Co., 1961.

Rooney, Richard P. "The Right Way to Pay." *Administrative Management* (October 1972):75–77.

Rothschild, William E. *Strategic Alternatives.* New York: AMACOM, 1979.

Schein, E. "On Organizational Culture." Research paper, M.I.T. Sloan School of Management, June 1981.

Schoeffler, S.; R.D. Buzzell; and D.F. Heany. "Impact of Strategic Planning on Profit Performance." *Harvard Business Review* (March-April 1974):137–145.

Schuster, Jay R. "A Spectrum of Pay for Performance." *Management of Personnel Quarterly* 8, no. 3 (Fall 1969).

Schuster, Jay R. "Executive Compensation: In the Eyes of the Beholder." *Business Horizons* VIII (April 1974):79–86.

Smyth, Richard C. *Financial Incentives for Management.* New York: McGraw-Hill, 1960.

Souder, William E. "One-Man Shows: Encouraging Entrepreneurship in the Large Corporations." *Research Management* (May 1981):18– .

Steers, Richard, and Lyman Porter. *Motivation and Work Behavior.* New York: McGraw-Hill, 1978.

Steiner, George A. *Strategic Planning.* New York: The Free Press, 1979.

Tannenbaum, Robert; I.K. Weschler; and F. Massarik. *Leadership and Organization: A Behavioral Science Approach.* New York: McGraw-Hill, 1961.

Tichy, Noel M.; Charles J. Fombrunt; and Mary Anne Devanna. "Strategic Human Resource Management." *Sloan Management Review* (Winter 1982):47–61.

Tourangeau, Kevin W. *Strategy Management.* New York: McGraw-Hill, 1981.

Tregoe, Benjamin B., and John W. Zimmerman. *Top Management Strategy.* New York: Simon and Schuster, 1980.

Treiman, Donald J., and Heidi I. Hartmann, eds. *Women, Work, and Wages: Equal Pay for Jobs of Equal Value.* Washington, D.C.: National Academy Press, 1981.

Vroom, Victor H., and Edward L. Deci. *Management and Motivation.* New York: Penguin Books, 1979.

Weeks, David A. "Compensating Employees: Lessons of the 1970's." *Report No. 707, The Conference Board Reports.* New York: The Conference Board, 1976.

Williams, Oliver F. "Business Ethics: A Trojan Horse?" *California Management Review* (Summer 1982):14–24.

Wilson, Michael. *Job Analysis for Human Resource Management: A Review of Selected Research and Development.* Manpower Research Monograph, no. 36. Washington, D.C.: U.S. Department of Labor, February 1974.

Wilson, Sidney R. "Motivating Managers with Money." *Business Horizons* (April 1973):37–43.

Index

About the Author

Jay Schuster received his B.B.A. and M.A. degrees from the University of Minnesota, and his Ph.D. from the University of Southern California. He is a managing principal at Sibson and Company, Inc., a subsidiary of Johnson and Higgins. He contributes to many business and academic journals and frequently speaks on organization performance.